The
HISPANIC
WAY

The HISPANIC WAY

Aspects of Behavior,

Attitudes, and Customs

in the Spanish-

Speaking World

JUDITH NOBLE · JAIME LACASA

PASSPORT BOOKS
NTC/Contemporary Publishing Group

cover photos
David Corona (Top right)
Robert Fried (Top left)
Kenji Kerins (Bottom right)

Published by Passport Books
An imprint of NTC/Contemporary Publishing Company
4255 West Touhy Avenue, Lincolnwood (Chicago), Illinois 60646-1975 U.S.A.

Contents

CONTENTS

INTRODUCTION

Different peoples have different languages and different values, beliefs, patterns of behavior, skills, habits, and the like—that is, different cultures. The culture traits of one people are not necessarily right or wrong, nor are they better or worse than those of others; they are simply different.

When we are interested in the people of another culture and would like to interact with them with a certain degree of ease, we have to learn what makes us alike and, perhaps more important, what makes us different. We have to learn about their environment and understand what they have received by societal tradition that we, of a different culture, have not.

Every culture is broad in scope and multifaceted. The various components of culture have been categorized traditionally under the headings of "big-c" culture and "little-c" culture.

"Big-c" culture is understood usually as the music, literature, and art of the people; it can be defined as what has been accumulated and passed down through the ages as the result of the creativity of the people. "Big-c" culture is everlasting, although the prominence of some of its elements can vary from time to time. It is the most frequently studied area of culture; it is a common focus of students of foreign languages. Its elements are very easy to find, and there is an abundance of written material about them—even in other disciplines, such as anthropology, sociology, art, and architecture. For the native, "big-c" culture is perhaps of greatest interest and the one to be emphasized when telling others of one's own culture.

INTRODUCTION

"Little-c" culture is a term whose concept and definition are varied. The authors consider "little-c" culture to comprise the elements that model people's behavior in daily interaction with one another and with society as a whole—elements that are subject to subtle change over time. For successful communication with the people of another culture, knowledge of their "little-c" culture is a requisite; lack of such knowledge can produce not only misunderstanding in any given act of communication, but also permanent disorientation, strain, and frustration—culture shock. Communication and understanding can be hindered to the extent that the foreigner totally rejects the new culture and its people. This, of course, is the exact opposite of the desired outcome of interaction with people of a different culture, which is to know them better and to appreciate them.

Many aspects of "little-c" culture are common knowledge; many are touched upon in Spanish language texts and in other books. However, a compilation of "little-c" culture traits common to the Hispanic world has heretofore been lacking. This book presents seventy-three points—a collection fairly exhaustive in scope and depth—of Hispanic "little-c" culture. It is designed to be a tool to aid in cultural enrichment and in the development of social fluency.

It must be remembered, given the geographical extension and variety to be found in the Hispanic world, that it is possible that not every generality will hold one hundred percent in every locale or in every instance. Nevertheless, the generalizations presented here are valid; an understanding of them and the ability to use the behaviorally oriented ones that are appropriate for a foreigner will broaden shared cultural knowledge, increase the quality of communication, help create a more comfortable feeling toward the Hispanic culture, and hopefully, ultimately make a step, no matter how small, toward greater worldwide understanding.

J. N.
J. L.
Iowa State University

1. ABBREVIATIONS AND ACRONYMS

Abbreviations

An abbreviation is a short form of a word or phrase and is usually, but not always, followed by a period. Some English abbreviations are:

p.	page
st.	street
NY	New York
sq. yd.	square yard

Spanish abbreviations *(abreviaturas)*

The most common abbreviations are part of the standard usage of the language and they can be found in various sources, such as the grammar of the Royal Spanish Academy. Some English-Spanish/Spanish-English dictionaries list abbreviations, either among the word entries or in separate sections. Other publications, such as catalogs, bibliographies, and encyclopedias, list the abbreviations that are used in the work.

Spanish words are abbreviated in two ways. A word may be abbreviated to its initial letter or to a few of its letters, which may or may not be contiguous. Abbreviations of proper nouns are capitalized; those of common nouns are usually written in lower-case:

Costa Rica	C. Rica
Argentina	Arg.
área	a.
página (page)	pág.
principal (main)	pral.
número (number)	n°

The abbreviation for a word in the plural can be its initial letter doubled (if the abbreviation of the singular is just the initial) or can end in *s* or *es* (if the abbreviation of the singular has more than one letter).

Fuerzas Armadas (Armed Forces)	FF. AA.
Estados Unidos (United States)	EE.UU.
páginas	págs.
principales	prales.
números	n^{os}

Some recognized abbreviations are capitalized to distinguish them from identical abbreviations, which are lower-cased:

autor (author)	A.	autores (authors)	AA.
área (area)	a.	áreas (areas)	aa.
decilitro	dl	decalitro	Dl
($^{1}/_{10}$ liter)		(10 liters)	

Some abbreviations can be written with capitals or lower-case letters, depending on custom:

S.S.S. and s.s.s can both be used for **su seguro servidor** (your true servant), a way of closing a letter.
F.C. and f.c. can both be used for **ferrocarril** (railway).

According to custom, some abbreviations are capitalized:

señor, señora, señorita	Sr., Sra., Srta.
(Mr., Mrs., Miss)	
señores (gentlemen, men and women, Mr. and Mrs.)	Sres.
usted (you, formal, singular)	Ud.
ustedes (you, formal, plural)	Uds.

Acronyms

An acronym is a word that is formed from the initial letters of the words of a descriptive phrase or a proper noun, or from the initial letters of the major components of a word. Acronyms are usually, but not always, written in all capital letters. Some English acronyms are:

scuba	self-contained underwater breathing apparatus
radar	radio detecting and ranging
NATO	North Atlantic Treaty Organization
OPEC	Organization of Petroleum Exporting Countries

Spanish *siglas*

Acronyms and other abbreviations formed by the initial letter or letters of a phrase are called *siglas* in Spanish. These, already numerous in Spanish, are increasing rapidly due mainly to the creation of new entities and institutions. One cannot read a newspaper or listen to the news without encountering them. While the older, more traditional acronyms are defined in dictionaries and elsewhere, it is often difficult or impossible to find the meanings of the more recent ones.

Some *siglas* are native to Hispanic culture. They are made from Spanish words or words from other languages spoken in Spain:

PRI	**Partido Revolucionario Institucional**
	Institutional Revolutionary Party
RENFE	**Red Nacional de los Ferrocarriles Españoles**
	National Network of Spanish Railroads
ETA	**Euzkadi Ta Azcatazuna**
	Land and Liberty (Basque)
C.F.P.C.	**Consell de Forces Polítiques de Catalonia**
(read **c-f-p-c**)	Council of Political Forces of Catalunya (Catalan)

Some *siglas* are borrowed from languages outside the Hispanic culture area. Of these, some are kept exactly as they are in the language of origin:

UNICEF	United Nations International Children's Emergency Fund
FAO	Food and Agriculture Organization
FBI	Federal Bureau of Investigation
(read **f-b-i**)	

3

Other *siglas* are transformations, reflecting the Spanish translation of the foreign phrase from which the original acronym was formed:

| OTAN | **Organización del Tratado del Atlántico Norte** (NATO) |
| SIDA | **Síndrome de Inmunización Adquirida** (AIDS) |

Gender and number of *siglas*

The gender and number of a *sigla* is usually dictated by the gender and number of the principal noun. Any article or other modifier has the same gender and number.

If the *sigla* is derived from Spanish words, the gender and number are that of the principal Spanish word:

el PRI	*el Partido* **Revolucionario Institucional** the Institutional Revolutionary Party
la COMIBOL	*la Corporación* **Minera Boliviana** the Bolivian Mining Corporation
las CC.OO.	*las Comisiones* **Obreras** the Workers' Commissions

However, a *sigla* that begins with a stressed *a* follows the rules of Spanish grammar, and requires the use of **el** instead of **la**:

| **el APRA** | *la Alianza* **Popular Revolucionaria Americana**
 American Popular Revolutionary Alliance |

If the *sigla* is derived from foreign words, but its meaning is easily understood, the gender is that of the Spanish equivalent of the principal word:

| **el FBI** | *el Buró* **Federal de Investigación** |
| **la CIA** | *la Agencia* **Central de Investigación** |

In other cases, the gender is dictated by the way the *sigla* sounds in Spanish, regardless of whether its origin is in Spanish or foreign words:

| **el YPFB** | **Yacimientos Petrolíferos Fiscales Bolivianos**
 Bolivian National Oil Fields |
| **la ETA** | **Euzkadi Ta Azcatazuna**
 Land and Liberty (Basque) |

Words developed from *siglas*

Nouns and adjectives have been derived from *siglas*:

APRA, for **Alianza Popular Revolucionaria Americana,** a Peruvian organization, gave rise to **aprista** as a noun (a member of this organization) and as an adjective (pertaining to or having the characteristics of the organization).

PRI, for **Partido Revolucionario Institucional,** gave rise to **priísta** as a noun and as an adjective.

ETA, for **Euzkadi Ta Azcatazuna,** Basque for Land and Liberty, gave rise to **etarra** as a noun and as an adjective.

INRI, for *Iesus Nazarenus Rex Iudeorum,* the Latin inscription on the cross on which Jesus was crucified, gave rise to the noun **inri,** meaning **dolor** (pain), **sufrimiento** (suffering), **burla** (scorn), **afrenta** (affront), as in **Su inri es su edad** (His age is the source of his suffering).

Reading/pronunciation of Spanish *siglas*

A *sigla* is usually read as a word if it sounds like a Spanish word:

> **FAO** borrowed from English for Food and Agriculture Organization

If a *sigla* does not sound like a Spanish word, it is usually read letter by letter:

> FBI is read **f–b–i;** PSOE is read **p–s–o–e.**

However, if the *sigla* is something of a tongue twister, the full name is often read if the meaning is known:

> **S.S.P.U.** (for **Servicio de Seguridad y Protección de los Portugueses de Ultramar,** Safety and Protection Service of Portuguese Abroad) would probably be read in its entirety.

If a *sigla* is in a foreign language and stands for something well known, the meaning may be given in its Spanish translation:

> USA may be read **Estados Unidos.**

❈

2. APPROACHING STRANGERS IN PUBLIC TO ASK SOMETHING

To ask for information, if possible, go to a significant person, such as a policeman, store clerk, waiter, or the like. (See Point 19, ''Directness.'') Be very polite. Greet the person with an appropriate phrase such as:

Perdón, señor . . .   Excuse me, sir . . .

Por favor . . .   Please . . .

Buenas tardes . . .   Good afternoon . . .

Then ask for what you want, using such phrases as:

¿Hay algo para mí?
Is there something for me?

¿Me puede ayudar?
Can you help me?

¿Podría ayudarme?
Would you be able to help me?

¿Me podría decir . . .?
Could you tell me . . .?

¿Tendría Ud. la bondad de . . .?
Would you be so kind as to . . .?

3. APRIL FOOL'S DAY

The first day of April has long been called April Fool's Day in our culture. The custom of playing tricks on this day is so old that its origin has been forgotten. Other cultures also observe certain times to play tricks on people.

The Spanish equivalent of April Fool's Day is December 28, **el día de los santos inocentes** (the day of the holy innocents, often referred to simply as **el día de los inocentes**), the day on which the Catholic Church commemorates the slaughter of the Holy Innocents by Herod. Tricks and pranks played on December 28 are called **inocentadas.** Even newspapers participate in the spirit of the day by publishing retouched photographs and altered ''news items.''

Although no one is sure why this date is celebrated by playing jokes on people, it may have to do with the meanings of the word **inocente**: "innocent," "blameless," "naive," and "foolish."

4. AT THE TABLE

Hands are never put in the lap; wrists or arms at mid-forearm rest on the edge of the table.

Silverware is used in the European way, with the fork in the left hand. When the fork is used to spear a piece of food, it is brought to the mouth with the tines down. During meals, knives and forks that are in use are placed utensil end on the plate (with the tines of the fork down), handle end on the table. To indicate that you have finished eating, place the silverware across the middle of the plate.

When you dine as a guest in a private home, leave a small amount on your plate when you have finished eating, or you may be served more. In a restaurant, if you still have a little food left on your plate, but seem to have finished eating, the waiter may well remove your plate without asking.

Although the whole meal may be a prolonged affair, each course is expected to be eaten fairly rapidly. When you finish a course, the next one may be brought to you, whether or not the others at the table are ready for their next course. You are expected to begin eating what has just been brought, not to wait for the rest of the people at the table to be served theirs.

Bread-and-butter plates are not common; diners often place their bread directly on the table, beside their plates. Serving dishes, condiments, and the like are not passed quite as much as in our culture; people reach for what is within reasonable distance. At meals with family and friends, it is not uncommon for salad to be served on one or more large platters in the center of the table, from which everyone eats directly. Similarly, in Valencia, Spain, where **paella** is the regional dish, a group of family members or close friends may eat directly from the **paellera,** the pan in which the **paella** was made.

5. ATTRACTING ATTENTION

¡**Perdón!** (Excuse me!) and **Por favor** (Please) can be used to attract someone's attention. They are used in speaking to people who are relatively close by. For people some distance away, you would use ¡**Oiga!**, ¡**Oigan!**, or ¡**Oye!**

¡**Oiga!** and ¡**Oigan!** are the singular (**Ud.**) and plural (**Uds.**) command forms of the verb **oír** (to hear). When they are used to attract attention, they more or less convey the idea of "Hey, there!" ¡**Oiga!** is used with an adult stranger or casual acquaintance:

¡**Oiga, camarero!**   Hey, there, waiter!

¡**Oigan!** is used when addressing more than one person:

¡**Oigan!** ¿**Es suyo esto?**   Hey, there! Is this yours?

¡**Oye!** is the informal singular (**tú**) command form of **oír.** It is used to attract the attention of a friend, a family member, a child, or a member of the household staff. It is also used to convey annoyance in speaking to adults with whom you would normally use the formal ¡**Oiga!** (See Point 66, "**Tú** and **usted, vosotros** and **ustedes.**")

| ¡**Oye!** ¡**Camarero!** | Hey, there! Waiter! (to the waiter who never comes) |
| ¡**Oye!** ¿**Qué haces?** | Hey, there! What are you doing? (to someone doing something you don't like, such as sitting on the hood of your car) |

¡**Señor!** (Sir!), ¡**Señora!** (Ma'am!), and ¡**Señorita!** (Miss!) may also be used to attract the attention of someone either close by or far away. If your intention is to ask for information or a favor, you should introduce the request with some polite word or phrase. (See Point 2, "Approaching strangers.")

Señor can be followed by the name of the person's occupation or role if he is of the same or higher social standing as the speaker.

¡**Señor guardia!**   Officer! (of the police or a similar force)

In bars and very informal restaurants, such as sidewalk cafes, the waiter may be called in ways that are not commonly used in our culture, such as clapping the hands twice; saying ¡pssst! once or twice; or tapping the side of a glass with the blade of a knife.

❁

6. "BAD LUCK" DAY

In our culture, Friday the thirteenth is considered by some to be a day of bad luck. The Spanish equivalent is Tuesday the thirteenth. In both cultures, some people believe that thirteen is an unlucky number, an idea that probably comes from the belief that there were thirteen disciples at the Last Supper, and that one was a traitor.

In the Hispanic world, **martes** (Tuesday) is considered by some an unlucky day, perhaps because the word comes from the name of Mars, the Roman god of war. There are even refrains that reflect this belief:

En martes, ni te cases ni te embarques.
On Tuesday, neither marry nor embark.

❁

7. BULLFIGHTING

The bullfight, **corrida de toros** or **fiesta brava,** is considered an art—**el arte del torco**—not a sport. Bullfighting is popular in Spain, parts of Hispanic America (mainly Mexico, Colombia, Peru, and Venezuela), Portugal, and southern France. In Spain, the bullfight is a major component of practically every festival of any importance; the **corrida de toros** is considered the most typical of all fiestas.

History

Some two thousand years before Christ, on the island of Crete, people participated in *taurokathapsia,* grasping a bull's horns and somersaulting over the animal. This activity, however, involved domesticated cattle.

9

Real bullfighting originated in the Iberian Peninsula, where the people contended with a different kind of animal *(Bos taurus Ibericus),* a spirited breed known to attack fiercely, even without provocation. During the Visigothic rule over the Iberian Peninsula (415–711), a popular spectacle featured the confrontation of man's brute strength with that of the bulls.

After the Moors invaded the peninsula in 711, they gradually modified the existing "bull games," incorporating into them their equestrian skills. A mounted master, lance in hand, fought the bull, while vassals on foot maneuvered the animal.

During the late Middle Ages, fighting bulls became chivalric tradition among both Christian and Moorish noblemen, who took the opportunity to exhibit not only their own magnificent equestrianism and their skill with short lances **(rejones),** but also the beauty of their well-trained horses. A remnant of this early style is still displayed by **rejoneadores,** mounted bullfighters who use the short lance.

From the late Middle Ages into the following centuries, it was not uncommon for kings and other members of royalty and nobility to enter the arena and fight bulls themselves. In 1567, as a result of frequent accidents and deaths (in 1512, more than ten knights were killed in a single **fiesta de toros**), Pope Pius V issued a papal edict in which he threatened to excommunicate princes who allowed bullfighting. The conquistadors brought bullfighting to the Americas in the early 1500s.

In the eighteenth century, bullfighting became a practice for professional bullfighters rather than for the nobility, and it began to be organized and regulated.

The first permanent bullring was built in Madrid in 1734. The present form of bullfighting dates from the nineteenth century.

Bullrings

The arena in which the bulls are fought—the bullring—is called **la plaza de toros.** This name has its origin in the **plaza** (square) where bullfights were originally held on festive occasions.

The best-known **plazas de toros** in Spain are **La Maestranza** in Seville, which is noted for its architectural beauty, and **La Monu-**

mental in Madrid, the largest in the country, with a capacity of 23,000. At this ring, a **novillero** (a novice bullfighter) who aspires to be a full-fledged **matador** must pass or reconfirm his official test of mastery, called **la alternativa.**

The largest of all **plazas de toros** in the world, with some 55,000 seats, is the **Plaza México** in Mexico City. This is also a site for **alternativas.**

Generalities

In Spain, the bullfighting season lasts from March to October. In Mexico, the season is from November to March; from April to October **novilladas** are presented (see below).

Bulls used in the **corrida** are special **toros de lidia** (fighting bulls). They are bred and raised for aggressive behavior, and solely for bullfighting, on special ranches called **ganaderías.** Each **ganadería** has its own colors **(divisas)** and, of course, its own brand.

A **novillada** is a **corrida** in which **novilleros** (novices), rather than full-fledged **toreros,** appear. They fight **novillos,** untamed bulls and cows of two or three years of age.

Toreros (a general term for anyone taking part in the fighting of bulls) wear the traditional **traje de luces** (suit of lights), a close-fitting silk suit with calf-length pants and a short jacket, both of which are embroidered with gold and/or silver and adorned with sequins. Completing this uniform are the **montera,** the flat, black, two-cornered hat, and black slippers.

Bulls are fought in different ways by the **toreros** and are killed (except in Portugal) by the principal **torero,** the **matador.** Each **corrida** comprises the facing of six bulls from the same **ganadería,** two each by a **matador** and his **cuadrilla** (crew). (If only two **matadores** are participating, regardless of the number of bulls to be fought, the **corrida** is called a **mano a mano**).

The bulls are assigned to each **matador** by lot. The senior **matador** fights the first and fourth bulls; the next in rank, the second and fifth bulls; the last, the third and sixth bulls. The fighting of each bull takes approximately twenty minutes.

11

Description of a bullfight

The **corrida** proceeds as follows:

A parade, called the **paseo,** begins the event. It is led by one or two men dressed in black, seventeenth-century costume, or by a celebrity, followed by all those who will participate in the bullfight, including the crew that removes the dead bulls from the ring (the **mulilleros**). A bull is released into the ring and is caped by the **peones,** the foot members of the **cuadrilla,** to study the behavior of the bull.

The **picadores** (lancers on horseback) jab the nape of the bull's neck to weaken the muscles that enable it to toss its head.

The **banderilleros** then place **banderillas** (pairs of darts about fifteen inches long, covered with colorful paper) in the nape of the bull's neck.

The **matador** (killer of the bull) capes the animal, which, when done skillfully, is a magnificent and colorful display of bravery. Finally, at **el momento de la verdad** (the moment of truth), he kills the bull instantaneously by thrusting his sword between the animal's shoulder blades and down through its heart.

During the bullfight, spectators show their approval of a good performance by applauding and by accompanying each **pase** (pass of the cape) with the rhythmic chanting of ¡Olé!

Once the bull has been killed, the people clamorously show their approval of the **matador,** sometimes by waving handkerchiefs. In cases of extreme disapproval of the **matador,** spectators may throw their rented seat cushions down into the arena.

If the **presidente,** the referee or judge of the performance of the **matadores,** agrees with the approval of the spectators, he waves his own white handkerchief to indicate that the **matador** is to be appropriately rewarded. Should the audience continue waving handkerchiefs and the **presidente** again concur, he signals for an additional award.

There are several possible awards. The lowest is **la vuelta al ruedo,** in which the **matador** is escorted around the arena by members of his **cuadrilla.** Then, according to the merit of his performance, the **matador** may be given one or more of the following: **oreja(s),** the ear(s) of the bull; **rabo,** the tail of the bull; **pata(s),** the hoof or hooves of the bull.

The **matador** then holds up his trophy or trophies to the spectators as he walks around the arena.

❁

8. BUSINESS

Business in general is often conducted on a more personal basis than
in our culture. A business conversation can shift quickly back and
forth from business to personal matters. Purely social visits are sometimes made to people at their places of business.

Business transactions are usually handled on a personal and sociable
level. This can be surprising and somewhat disconcerting to someone
from another culture who is used to a very direct, straightforward, fairly
fast-moving way of conducting business. On the other hand, our "busi-
nesslike" approach might seem brusque or even quite rude to someone in
the Hispanic world. (See Point 70, "Way of conveying information.")

Businesses are often family enterprises run by father, sons, and at
times, other more distant family members. Hiring relatives is a commonly accepted practice, related to strong family ties and the function of
the extended family in society. This is particularly intense in times of
high unemployment. (See Point 26, "Family and friends.")

Merchandising, in decreasing degree from the market vendor to
the clerk in a chain store, serves a social function as well as a commercial one in the vendor's society. In some instances, the social importance of merchandising is greater than the commercial one.

Business hours

There is great freedom in opening and closing times. At any time, any
day, the person in charge may decide to close the establishment. During "normal" working hours, it is not uncommon to see signs such as
Cerrado hoy (Closed today) and **Cerrado esta tarde** (Closed this
afternoon) on the door of a store or office.

Stores, banks, the post office, and many other government offices (from local to national) close for a few hours in the early afternoon, then resume business and stay open until early evening. (See

Point 40, "Meals and meal times.") However, some banks and government offices, especially during the summer, may have a **jornada intensiva** (an intensive workday), uninterrupted by the traditional midday closing, and ending earlier than usual.

Particularly in Spain, most people vacation in July and August. During this time, there is great variety in business hours and days. Establishments may be open only in the morning, closed certain days, open from three to five on one day and four to six on another. Schedules may be posted to indicate business hours.

Saturday is generally a regular workday, but the **semana inglesa** (English week)—the five- or five-and-a-half-day work week—is becoming more popular. Many stores and offices now post notices saying whether they are open on Saturday.

Everything is closed on Sunday, as well as on religious, national, and local holidays. Even the post office, which is part of the national system, may close on local holidays.

Some establishments, such as pharmacies, which provide semi-emergency services, take turns being open twenty-four hours a day or on days when they would normally be closed. The store that is open is called **de turno** or **de guardia,** as in **la farmacia de turno** or **la farmacia de guardia.** The ones that are closed will have a notice posted indicating the name and address of the **de turno/de guardia** establishment in that area, or a schedule telling when each of several establishments are **de turno/de guardia.** These schedules might also be announced in local newspapers.

❁

9. CALENDAR

The first day of the Hispanic week is **lunes,** Monday. In our culture, we count periods of one and two weeks by weeks. In Hispanic culture, they are counted by days, and include both the beginning and ending days. The result is that a week is represented as eight days, and two weeks are represented as fifteen days:

Salimos en ocho días.
We're leaving in a week (eight days).

Salimos en quince días.
We're leaving in two weeks (fifteen days).

Salimos en tres semanas.
We're leaving in three weeks.

Salimos de hoy en ocho días.
We're leaving a week from today (from today in eight days).

Salimos de hoy en quince días.
We're leaving two weeks from today (from today in fifteen days).

Salimos de hoy en tres semanas.
We're leaving three weeks from today (from today in three weeks).

Pasamos ocho días allí.
We spent a week (eight days) there.

Pasamos quince días allí.
We spent two weeks (fifteen days) there.

Pasamos tres semanas allí.
We spent three weeks there.

In the Hispanic world, the full date is written in a different order from the way we do it: first the number of the day, then the month, then the year. The measures of time go from the smallest (the day) to the next in size (the month) to the largest (the year).

April 30, 1992   **30 de abril, 1992**

If the date is expressed in figures only, a Roman numeral is usually used for the month:

April 30, 1992 (4/30/92)   **30/IV/92** or **30/4/92**

10. CALLING CARDS

Calling cards, **tarjetas de visita,** are used much more commonly in the Hispanic world than they are in our culture. Businesspeople may have cards that they use in social situations, as well as in their business dealings.

Recent university graduates may have calling cards with their name, degree (**Licenciado** or **Licenciada en química,** for example), address, and phone number.

❁

11. CASUAL ENCOUNTERS

In our culture, if we are out alone in public and encounter a total stranger who is also alone, we may smile and say ''Hi!'' or otherwise casually greet the person. This might happen, for instance, when we pass someone on campus, when we get into an elevator with one person already in it, when we open a door to enter an office and find someone on the other side who was about to open the door to leave, when we walk past a grocery store employee who is stocking shelves, or while waiting for a bus. We might have a brief chat about something like the weather or what time the next bus will be along.

Our behavior could stem from our not really paying attention to the person we greet in any impersonal one-on-one situation. We might just be reacting nervously to a situation in which we feel some obligation to say something lest we appear rude. But in a different situation, we may not recognize the person we greeted, may not even be aware that he or she is there, or simply may not feel the same need to say or do anything.

In the Hispanic world, behavior of this kind, especially on the part of a woman, would startle people. While a Hispanic might be surprised by such a casual demonstration of friendliness by a stranger, he or she would be even more surprised and even disappointed if the friendly behavior were not repeated the next time a casual meeting took place.

To a Hispanic, a person who demonstrates a degree of friendliness at one time is expected to show the same degree of familiarity (no matter how limited) in further contacts. Because of this attitude, a

simple, casual smile, greeting, comment, or gesture by a female—
something that might be very natural in our culture and have no implications or overtones whatever—could be interpreted by a Hispanic
as the beginning of something and as very forward behavior.

❈

12. CELEBRATIONS AND HOLIDAYS

Fiesta, when it means "party," does not necessarily refer to a
friendly get-together, as it might when we use the word *party*. **Fiesta**
usually means a rather elaborate celebration, a truly festive event. It
means more truly a festival or a party in celebration of something. For
instance, **mañana es día de fiesta** means "tomorrow is a holiday (religious or secular)."

The term **fiesta nacional** refers to an official national holiday;
las fiestas refers to festivals—local, regional, or national—that may
be held only one day or may last several days.

Most holidays (**días de fiesta** or **días feriados**) in the Hispanic
world are centered around or have their origins in religion, and many
celebrations of the Catholic Church are officially designated by gov-
ernments as holidays. However, in countries where the government is
leaning toward secularization, some traditional religious holidays are
losing their official status.

While some holidays, such as Christmas, are universal and can
be anticipated, many local, regional, and national ones (and they are
abundant) can catch a foreigner by surprise. Even the known holidays
will almost certainly be observed differently from the way to which the
visitor is accustomed.

National government offices, such as the post office, may be
closed or have limited hours for local or regional holidays. And even
at times of religious holidays, the business world, to some extent, may
come to a halt; stores and banks may be closed or have limited hours.
Three of the best-known holidays of the Hispanic world take place in
Spain—**las Fiestas de San Fermín, las Fallas de San José,** and **la
Feria de Sevilla.** (See below.)

Religious celebrations

The main religious celebrations in the Hispanic world are:

Epifanía or **Día de los Reyes Magos**	January 6, Epiphany *or* Day of the Magi, Day of the Wise Men
Miércoles de Ceniza	Ash Wednesday .
Domingo de Ramos	Palm Sunday
Jueves Santo	Maundy (Holy) Thursday
Viernes Santo	Good Friday
Día de Pascua	Easter[1]
Corpus Christi	Festival honoring the Eucharist (the consecrated bread used in Holy Communion), held the Thursday after Trinity Sunday (the Sunday following Whitsunday or Pentecost, which is the seventh Sunday or the fiftieth day after Easter). In many places, **Corpus Christi** is celebrated with public processions. The most spectacular observances are held in Toledo and Granada, in Spain.
Día de Todos los Santos	All Saints' Day, November 1 (The word *Halloween* means ''saints''' or ''hallows' day eve,'' the Eve of All Saints' Day.) Although Halloween is not observed in the Hispanic world, the Spanish for *Halloween* is **Víspera de Todos los Santos.**

---

[1]The word **pascua,** which is used in the designation of several different religious holidays, comes from the Latin *pascha,* and that from the Hebrew *pesach,* which means ''sacrifice for the people's immunity.'' The term **pascua** is used to designate the following religious holidays: **Pascua de los hebreos** (Passover); **Pascua, Pascua de Resurrección, Pascua florida, Pascua de flores, Día de Pascua** (Easter); **Pascua del Espíritu Santo** (Pentecost, the seventh Sunday after Easter, commemorating the Holy Spirit's appearance to the Apostles); **las Pascuas, las Pascuas de Navidad** (any of the events related to Christmas, from December 25 [observance of the birth of Christ] through January 6 [Epiphany, the arrival of the Wise Men].)
Felices Pascuas means ''Merry Christmas''; **Feliz Día de Pascua** means ''Happy Easter.''

Día de Todos los Fieles Difuntos, Día de los Muertos	All Souls' Day (Day of All the Faithful Dead; Day of the Dead), November 2
Nochebuena	Christmas Eve, December 24
Día de Navidad	Christmas, December 25

In addition, each country, region, city, and town has its own patron saint. The festivities, both religious and secular, that honor these saints **(fiestas patronales)** may last more than one day, and usually culminate on the day of the calendar assigned to the particular saint. The most universal religious celebrations in the Hispanic world are Christmas **(Navidad)** and Holy Week **(Semana Santa),** followed by Easter **(Día de Pascua)** and, in many places, the Day of the Dead **(Día de Todos los Fieles Difuntos** or **Día de los Muertos).**

Navidad

Christmas in Spanish is **Navidad, Navidades,** or **Pascuas (de Navidad).** (For **Pascuas,** see the footnote on page 18.) Although customs vary from country to country, and even from region to region, Christmas is celebrated throughout the Hispanic world. The day before Christmas, Christmas Eve, in Spanish is **la víspera de Navidad;** the night of Christmas Eve is **Nochebuena.** The midnight mass said on **Nochebuena** is called **misa del gallo** (mass of the rooster). During the Christmas season, traditional carols, **villancicos,** are usually sung.

There are few Christmas trees in private homes; much more common is the **nacimiento** (birth), or **belén** (from **Belén,** Bethlehem), an elaborate nativity scene, or a simpler manger scene or group of figures called a **pesebre.**

The most notable difference between the Hispanic celebration and that of our culture is that in many places gifts are not exchanged on December 25. Instead they are ''brought'' (usually only for children) on January 6 by the **Reyes Magos** (the Three Wise Men), **Melchor, Gaspar,** and **Baltasar.** Children put hay out on balconies or on window sills for the Wise Men's mounts (two horses and a camel), then place their shoes near the hay for the presents to be placed in. Children are warned before the Christmas season that if they don't behave, the **Reyes Magos** will leave coal instead of gifts.

Las posadas

During the Christmas season, especially in Mexico, **las posadas** (the lodgings), which represent Mary and Joseph's journey from Nazareth to Bethlehem and their search for a place to stay, begin on December 16 and end on Christmas Eve (December 24).

The origin of the **posadas** is an Aztec ceremony adapted for part of the observation of Christmas by Fray Diego de Soria, the prior of the monastery at Acolmán, Mexico.

One family usually organizes the **posadas,** and offers its home either for each of the nine **posadas** or for only the last one. Eight other families are invited to host the first eight **posadas,** at their own homes or at the home of the organizing family, which always hosts the last **posada**.

The people involved in the **posadas,** relatives and friends, adults and children, are divided into groups. One group is made up of the pilgrims, who go by candlelight procession, at eight or nine o'clock in the evening, to the house of the **posada** to ask for shelter. The second group occupies the house to which the procession goes. The pilgrims stop in front of the house and sing a song, begging for shelter. The man representing Joseph and the **posada** host, who represents the innkeeper, carry on a conversation in verse. There are differing versions of their song; the following is one variation.

Joseph asks for lodging:

En nombre del cielo	In the name of heaven
os pido posada	I ask you for lodging
pues no puede andar	for she cannot go on
mi esposa amada.	my beloved wife.

The innkeeper refuses:

Aquí no es mesón.	This is not an inn.
Sigan adelante.	Go on your way.
Yo no puedo abrir,	I cannot open,
no sea algún tunante.	lest you be a scoundrel.

Joseph insists:

No seas inhumano.	Don't be inhumane.
Tennos caridad,	Take pity on us,
que el Dios de los cielos	for the God of the heavens
te lo premiará.	will reward you for it.

The innkeeper angrily replies:

Ya se pueden ir	Now you can go away
y no molestar,	and not bother (me),
porque si me enfado	because if I get angry
los voy a apalear.	I'm going to beat you all with a stick.

Finally, the innkeeper realizes the importance of the travelers and lets them in. Now the tone changes, and the people in the house sing:

Entren, santos peregrinos, peregrinos,	Enter, holy pilgrims, pilgrims,
Reciban este rincón,	Receive this corner,
no de esta pobre morada, pobre morada,	not of this humble house, humble house,
sino de mi corazón.	but of my heart.

After the people enter, refreshments are served. The culmination of the festivities of each evening is the breaking of the **piñata** (see below). A child or adult is blindfolded and given a stick. He or she tries to hit the elusive **piñata,** which is held high and constantly moved out of reach. Finally, someone is allowed to break it, and there is a scramble for the contents (candies and small toys).

The house of a **posada** displays a **nacimiento** with a simulated landscape of Bethlehem. Each night the statues of Joseph and Mary are moved, reaching the manger on December 24. Then, at the ninth **posada,** the statue of the baby Jesus is "rocked to sleep" and "godparents" are chosen for Him from among the guests. The "godparents" will sponsor the **posada** of January 6, which represents the visit of the Three Wise Men to the manger. Among the responsibilities of the January 6 hosts will be providing presents for the guests.

The **posadas,** usually regarded as a Mexican celebration, have become a part of the Christmas observance in some places in the

United States: the San Luis Rey Mission in the Old Town section of San Diego, California; in Sante Fe, New Mexico; in San Antonio, Texas; and in Chicago, Illinois.

La piñata

The **piñata** was originally a clay pot or similar container filled with candy and suspended from the ceiling at a masked ball held on the first Sunday of Lent. Guests were blindfolded and given a cane or a pole, which they swung at the **piñata** in an effort to break it.

Present-day **piñatas** are colorful containers, usually made of papier-mâché or lightweight cardboard, in a variety of shapes (animals, stars, boats, sometimes even people). They are covered with long strips of colored tissue paper that have been folded and partially cut crosswise. The uncut edges are glued to the figure, giving a fringe-like appearance over the surface of the **piñata.**

Piñatas are popular in Mexico for the celebration of children's saints' days, birthdays, and other celebrations, such as *posadas.*

Semana Santa

Holy Week is marked in many places by large, elaborate religious processions in which, especially in Spain, hooded men, clad in tunics, carry or accompany statues (of Christ or the Virgin Mary) or **pasos.** **Pasos** are very ornate platforms, similar to floats, bearing a representation of one of the stages of the Passion. They are borne on the shoulders of several men.

Each **paso** belongs to a **cofradía** (confraternity) connected with a parish church. **Los cofrades,** the members of each **cofradía,** march in procession with their **paso** during Holy Week, usually on Good Friday. The most famous **Semana Santa** observances take place in Seville and Valladolid, Spain.

Semana Santa in Seville

Semana Santa in Seville is a magnificent week-long religious observation and performance. James A. Michener called it "the world's
most profound religious spectacle."[2]

According to tradition, the celebration of Holy Week in Seville
began in the fourteenth century with a procession called **Santo En-
tierro** (Holy Burial). Near the end of that century, in 1380, two more
processions were added, the **Vera-Cruz** (the True Cross) and the
Santo Crucifijo (the Holy Crucifix).

Over the years, the processions have grown in importance and
the **cofradías** and the **pasos** have increased in number. Today there
are fifty-two **cofradías** and more than a hundred **pasos.** Each **cofradía** has special shouted commands that are used for starting and
stopping the procession and raising and lowering the **pasos.** Only the
cofrades of each specific **cofradía** understand its commands.

Most of the statues of Christ and Mary and those in the **pasos** are
works of art from the seventeenth century. Many were created by the
famous Spanish sculptors **Juan Martínez Montañés** (1568–1649)
and **Pedro Roldán** (1624–1700).

Several statues are outstanding for their beauty and for their
number of devotees: **la Macarena,** "(Our Lady of) the Macarena"
after **La Macarena,** a popular neighborhood in Seville; **la Esperanza
Trianera,** "(Our Lady of) the Hope of Triana," named after
Triana, the famous gypsy quarter of Seville; **el Cristo de los Gita-
nos,** "the Christ of the Gypsies"; **el Jesús de la Pasión,** "Jesus of the
Passion"; **el Jesús del Gran Poder,** "Jesus of the Great Power."

The color of the tunics and hoods worn by the **cofrades** are symbolic. Black represents death; red, blood and suffering; white, scorn
for the world; green, hope; purple, penance.

The Holy Week atmosphere in Seville is characterized by the
smell of the burning wax of the tall candles **(cirios)** carried by the **cofrades.** There are characteristic sounds, too—the sound of the **bas-
tones de mando** (batons of authority) hitting the ground; the slow religious music; the dragging of the penitents' chains; the voices of the

---

[2]Michener, James A. *Iberia.* New York: Random House, 1968, p. 263.

command of **Arriba, al cielo con ella** ("Up, to the sky with it," *it* referring to the **anda,** the platform on which the **paso** rests), with which the **capataz** (leader of the carriers of the **pasos**) directs the maneuvering of the heavy **pasos** through the streets. The most emotional sound is that of the **saetas.** A **saeta** is a type of short, moving, moralizing ballad **(copla)**, which is often improvised, and whose characteristic rhythm and sound reflect its Arabic origin. **Saetas** usually allude to the sufferings of the Virgin Mary and of Christ and are sung during the processions of **Semana Santa** to move the audience to devotion.

Día de los Muertos (Day of the Dead)

This is an important day for observance in different ways and degrees in the Hispanic world. It is a common tradition to visit cemeteries and decorate the graves of family and loved ones with flowers and wreaths. (In Mexico City, yellow and gold marigold-like **flores de los muertos,** flowers of the dead, are the preferred flowers for this ritual.) In some places, the visit to the cemetery includes a picnic at the gravesite.

In many places, people attend the theater to see a performance of the famous *Don Juan Tenorio* by the noted Spanish playwright, **José Zorrilla** (1817–1893).

There are many other ways this day is observed. In Mexico, for instance, bakers prepare special loaves of bread—**pan de muerte,** bread of death—in different shapes, such as corpses or long bones. Confectioners make assorted sizes of **calaveras** (skulls made of sugar). Children delight in toys symbolic of death—miniature hearses, skeletons, small dolls in a funeral procession, tiny altars with offerings for the dead, and "dancing" skeletons on poles.

Fiestas in Spain

La Feria de Sevilla

The **Feria de Sevilla** is a fair that follows the Holy Week celebration. It normally takes place two weeks following Easter, unless that would put it in May, in which case the celebration is advanced. This is probably the most famous and important fair in all Europe, and there are those who think the **Feria de Sevilla** is THE reason to visit Spain. A huge park, near and to the south of the center of Seville, is divided into three separate but connected areas that form the site of the **feria.** One area is for circuses and, during the week, as many as five world-famous circuses perform simultaneously. The adjoining area is for the carnival, a sea of rides, games, shooting galleries, and outdoor restaurants, all of which operate twenty-four hours a day. (A characteristic food of the fair is **churros,** deep-fried fritters dusted with powdered sugar.) This area is noted for its extremely high noise level, caused by numerous and competing loudspeakers. The third sector, which attracts the greatest number of visitors, is filled with private **casetas,** little house frames with wooden floors and bright striped canvas walls and roofs. The **casetas,** which are built especially for the occasion, are opened by rolling up the front canvas. Each **caseta** has running water, many lights, a large table, and some two dozen chairs. Here the well-to-do Sevillians spend most of their time at the fair, returning home for the few hours between 5:00 and 11:00 A.M. to get some sleep.

When the owners are at their **casetas,** invited guests join the family for **churros** and sherry or other refreshments, accompanied by flamenco music and dancing.

Aside from the small private **casetas,** there are some large ones. Some are private, but others are open to the public, and anyone can pay to see flamenco dancing and have something to drink. Among the large private **casetas** is the outstanding and famous one belonging to the **Aero Club,** whose members and guests are of the highest echelon of Spanish society.

Every day during the **feria,** beginning at noon and lasting some three hours, there is an informal ''parade'' of members of high Sevillian society. Men and women on horseback, some dressed in the beautiful and colorful Andalusian costumes, ride up and down the **Real de la Feria,** the men riding in front in the saddle, the women sitting sidesaddle on pillions behind them. At times, they stop to chat or have a drink, without dismounting; at other times, they dismount and join people who have invited them into their **casetas.** Others in this informal parade are people in elaborately adorned carriages, who participate in the festivities in similar fashion.

Las Fallas

This is the week of festivities held throughout the autonomous region of Valencia (the provinces of Castellón, Valencia, and Alicante), but mainly in the city and province of Valencia. **Las fallas** (in Valencian **les falles**) begin on March 12 and end on March 19, **el día de San José** (the day of Saint Joseph), the feast day of the patron saint of carpenters and other woodworkers.

This celebration seems to have originated in the sixteenth century. Each fall, as the days grew shorter, in order to be able to continue working, carpenters built wooden stands to hold lights. The stand (in Valencian called **parot** or **estai**) had a kind of tripod base and, close to the top, a horizontal bar that held the torches, candles, or other means of illumination. In the spring, as the days grew longer, the use of the light stands was no longer necessary. On March 18, the eve of the day honoring their patron, Saint Joseph, carpenters and other woodworkers cleaned shop in anticipation of the celebration, piling wood chips, scraps, and other useless pieces by the stands and setting the whole thing on fire.

At some point, someone had the idea of dressing the **parot** with old clothes, creating the first **ninot.** (**Ninot** is the Valencian word for a life-size or larger figure that forms part of a **falla.** See below.) Later on, **ninots** became caricatures of well-known people, a tradition still followed today. The first-known ''real'' **falla** was in 1538. The present festivities center around neighborhood **fallas,** which are best described as elaborate immobile parade floats made up of larger-than-life-size figures **(ninots)** and painted scenes, all fashioned out of cardboard, papier-mâché, and wood. The figures and scenes are usually criticisms of current social situations and events. (The male members of a **falla** group are **fallers,** the females are **falleres.**) The organizers and other people in charge of each group make up the **comissió.** Each year, the **comissió** publishes a **llibret,** a booklet explaining the meaning and symbolism of the group's **falla.** Each **falla,** which has been under construction for most of the year, is erected midweek in a plaza or in a side intersection in the neighborhood. The erecting of the **fallas** (**la plantá** in Valencian) is done more or less secretly, in the dark of the night. The following day, everyone goes around town to see the competing **fallas.** The **fallas** are judged, and prizes are awarded to the best ones. Each neighborhood with a **falla** hires a full-scale band that parades through the streets of the town, day and night, during the week. The week-long celebration is highlighted by street dances and fireworks at night. On the night of March 19 (**la nit de foc,** Valencian for "the night of fire"), the **fallas** are burned (**la cremá**). However, the best **ninot, ninot indultat,** is spared, and in some places it is saved and preserved in a **fallas** museum. When the **fallas** are burned, all but the one that received the first prize (and, of course, the **ninot indultat**) are set on fire at the same time. Once they have been consumed by the flames, everyone gathers around the first-prize winner and witnesses its burning.

Las Fiestas de San Fermín **or** los sanfermines

This is a well-known week-long celebration that takes place in the northern city of Pamplona, Spain, the capital of the autonomous community of Navarra. It begins on July 6, for the observance of the day of **San Fermín,** and continues for several days. **Las Fiestas de San Fermín** receive media attention even in the United States because of **el encierro,** the famous "running of the bulls," which were popularized by Ernest Hemingway in his novel *Fiesta.* The festivities begin at the City Hall, immediately after the last stroke of the clock at noon on July 6, with the **chupinazo,** the firing of a fireworks mortar, followed by the shout of ¡**Viva San Fermín!** (Long live San Fermin!), to which the crowd responds enthusiastically ¡**Viva!** Each morning the activities begin at eight o'clock sharp (the town is very proud of its punctuality) with **el encierro,** the running of the bulls. The bulls that are to be fought that afternoon are released from the corral and allowed to run through the blocked-off streets (one of which is the well-known **calle de la Estafeta**) that guide them to the **plaza de toros** (bullring), where they are locked up in the **toriles** (bull pens). Young men, usually dressed in the traditional **San Fermín** garb of white shirt and pants, red bandanna around the neck, and red sash around the waist, show off their courage and daring by running ahead of the bulls. On occasion, participants are wounded; at times, mortally.

Once the bulls are in the **toriles,** the bull pens adjoining the ring, **vaquillas emboladas,** young cows with their horns capped with wooden balls for safety, are let loose in the ring for the general entertainment of spectators who want to get into the ring with them.

Following the **encierro,** the city is quiet, and people sleep until noon. Then they are awakened by the sound of the **dulzainas** (a type of recorder) that accompanies the **gigantes** and **cabezudos,** who wind their way, at times dancing, through the streets of the city. This is a spectacle that evokes excitement in children and adults alike. (The **gigantes** are two people dressed in very tall costumes; one is a king, the other a queen. The **cabezudos** are several people dressed in costumes with enormous heads.)

People eat late in the afternoon, then go to the bullring for the bullfight. **Peñas,** groups of young male friends, often with their after-dinner cigars in their mouths, march off in the direction of the bullring. It has been said that during the bullfight, the activity in the **tendidos** (the tiers of seats in the stands at a bullring) is as interesting as that in the **ruedo** (bullring arena).

When the bullfight is over, the **peñas** leave the bullring, dancing and jumping to the rhythm of the **jotas. Jota,** in the Aragonese dialect of Spanish, is the name of a dance, the music that accompanies the dance, and the lyrics sung to the **jota** melody. **Jotas** are popular in the regions of Aragón, Navarra, and Valencia, Spain.

The festivities continue all night long until just before it is time for the **encierro** of the next morning, when the celebrants have the traditional snack of **sopa de ajo,** a cold garlic soup made of mashed raw garlic, bread crumbs, salt, olive oil, vinegar, water, and, occasionally, crushed almonds.

These activities are repeated daily for a week.

Other celebrations

The most common secular celebration throughout the Hispanic world is the **Día de la Raza** (Day of the Race), October 12 (Columbus Day in the United States), observing the anniversary of the discovery of America by **Cristóbal Colón** (Christopher Columbus) in 1492 and recognizing the common bonds that unite the people of the Hispanic world.

In the Americas, the **Día de las Américas** is celebrated on April 14. Throughout the Hispanic world, there is a variety of secular and civic observances and holidays, including **Día de la Bandera** (Flag Day), **Día del Maestro** (Teacher's Day), **Día de las Fuerzas Armadas** (Armed Forces Day), and **Día de la Madre** (Mother's Day). **Noche Vieja** (New Year's Eve, literally "Old Night") and **Día de Año Nuevo** (New Year's Day) are also observed.

Practically everywhere in the Hispanic world, in varying degrees and ways, **Carnaval** (Carnival), the equivalent of our Mardi Gras, is celebrated. **Carnaval** refers to the three days that precede **el miércoles de ceniza** (Ash Wednesday), although the length of the observance may vary. The word **carnaval** comes to Spanish from the Italian word *carnevale,* from the Latin *carnem levare* (to remove the meat), which refers to the earlier tradition of removing meat from the diet during **Cuaresma** (Lent), which begins on Ash Wednesday.

There is one universal civic holiday, the **Día de la Independencia** (Independence Day), celebrated in each country according to its own tradition. This observance is called **fiestas patrias** (festivities celebrating the **patria,** fatherland/motherland), and may last more than one day.

Country	Independence Day	Country	Independence Day
Argentina	July 9	Guatemala	September 15
Bolivia	August 6	Honduras	September 15
Chile	September 18	Mexico	September 16
Colombia	July 20	Nicaragua	September 15
Costa Rica	September 15	Panama	November 28 (from Spain)
Cuba	May 20		November 3 (from Colombia)
Dominican Republic	February 22	Paraguay	May 14
Ecuador	October 3	Peru	July 28
El Salvador	September 15	Uruguay	August 25
Equatorial Guinea	October 12	Venezuela	July 5

Spain has a **Día de la Independencia,** May 2, commemorating the uprising in 1808 against the invasion by Napoleon's troops, but this is not a holiday. There is a national holiday, **Fiesta Nacional,** October 12, which was established recently.

❁

13. THE COLOR BROWN

The Spanish language is very discriminatory in how something is labeled as brown in color. There are several words that translate as *brown*. They are not interchangeable, and each one is used to describe certain things: **marrón** describes man-made things; **castaño** describes eye or hair color; **pardo** usually describes animals and things in nature.

Of course, **de color café**, or simply **café**, covers a multitude of hues, considering the color of very weak coffee, of very strong coffee, and of something in between.

❁

14. COMMANDS AND STATEMENTS IN DISTRIBUTION OF TASKS

One may be addressed with a command form of a verb or with a flat statement, often with a verb in the future tense, which may be interpreted by the non-Hispanic as a very brusque mandate. Actually, unless the tone of voice indicates otherwise, this is very often merely a way of distributing tasks. For example, while getting ready for a party, someone could say to one person:

> **Ve y compra el queso mientras yo arreglo la sala.**
> Go and buy the cheese while I straighten up the living room.

to another:

> **Y tú, prepara los bocadillos cuando él regrese.**
> And you, fix the sandwiches when he gets back.

or to the first person:

Tú irás y comprarás el queso y yo arreglaré la sala.
You will go and buy the cheese and I will straighten up the living room.

to the other:

Y tú, prepararás los bocadillos cuando él regrese.
And you will fix the sandwiches when he gets back.

❖

15. COMPLIMENTS, ADMIRATION, APPRECIATION, AND GRATITUDE

If someone compliments you, it is considered brash to answer with only **Gracias** (Thank you) or **Muchas gracias** (Thank you very much) because such an answer may imply that you think you deserve the compliment. The appropriate response to a compliment is to say that the person is very kind or that you are glad that the person likes whatever was complimented. For example:

Ud. está muy elegante esta noche.
You are very elegant tonight.
> **Ud. es muy amable.**
> You are very kind.

Ud. habla muy bien el español.
You speak Spanish very well.
> **Gracias. Ud. es muy amable.**
> Thank you. You are very kind.

Está muy bueno. Me gusta mucho. Ud. es muy buena cocinera.
It's very good. I like it a lot. You are a very good cook.
> **Me alegro que le guste.**
> I'm glad that you like it.
> > or
>
> **Ud. es muy amable.**
> You are very kind.

Don't show excessive admiration of something that belongs to someone else, even if you do so to praise the owner, lest that person feel an obligation to give it to you.

People may not be as effusive in expressing gratitude for a gift or for a gesture of kindness, or as apt to recall such things at a future date, as might be expected in our culture.

❇

16. CONVENTIONALISM

In the Hispanic world, rudeness or failure to observe basic good manners is viewed much more critically than in our culture. Society is more restrained, conservative, and traditional, with more attention paid to conventions of behavior. People are more concerned with and place more emphasis on **el que dirán** (what they will say). There are more don'ts in Hispanic culture than in ours, with ''violations'' much more frowned upon.

Generally, behavior in public places such as offices is not as casual as it can be in our culture. People do not put their feet on a desk **(la línea Hollywood)**; they never stretch or lean back in a chair in a stretching posture; they do not sit or perch on a desk or table. In a crowded airport or railroad or bus station, no one sits on the floor. (You might see people sitting or even sleeping on the floor, but they are usually foreigners or young nationals traveling in a group.) Men do not stand or walk with their hands in their pockets. In restaurants, people do not figure up and pay their portion of the check. This would be a source of great shock and consternation to those witnessing it.

Mourning conventions are much stronger and more extended than in our culture. The dress code is black first, and later other dark colors; men wear black armbands. ''Fun'' activities (parties, movies, etc.) are forbidden or very restricted. The length of mourning depends on the closeness of the deceased to the mourner and the age of the deceased: mourning for a parent, spouse, or sibling is longer than for uncles and cousins; mourning for adults is longer than for children. One year of ''full'' mourning is not uncommon.

❇

17. CONVERSATIONS

Conversations between Hispanics can be very loud, fast, and punctuated with many gestures. People may raise their voices, but not necessarily in anger; very often it is done to better convey a point. More than one person may talk at the same time, and people may interrupt one another, starting to talk before the speaker has finished. In informal conversation, animated or not, this is not considered rude or disrespectful. In fact, at times, someone's failure to interrupt could be taken as a sign of the person's lack of interest in the speaker or in what is being said.

�

18. DATING AND MARRIAGE

Although they are changing, traditional customs that differ from those of our culture still exist.

Group co-ed activities begin at about age fourteen, the important word here being *group*. Major forms of entertainment are attending movies, dances, sporting events, parties at someone's home; strolling around plazas, parks, or other public areas where people gather for social purposes; or going on picnics. Real dating is more restricted and doesn't begin until age eighteen or nineteen; pairing off is usually done only if marriage is being considered.

A man still asks a woman's father for her hand in marriage. Parents and other relatives of a couple exert a very strong influence in the acceptance of the proposed marriage partner, because any newcomer to the family becomes a part of the extended family. (See Point 26, ''Family and friends.'') Engagements of several years are common. Since couples usually do not marry until the man has finished his education, fulfilled any military obligation, and established himself financially, the average marrying age for men is twenty-seven, for women twenty to twenty-four.

In many places, a civil ceremony, which is necessary for the marriage to be legally recognized, is held before the religious one. Newlyweds often live with the family of the bride or the groom until they are able to afford a place of their own. (See Point 26, ''Family and friends.'')

❈

19. DIRECTNESS

In some parts of Spanish America, especially the Andean countries (Ecuador, Peru, and Bolivia), people who are frank, open, and direct are considered rude and blunt. In some places, people who feel that the one speaking to them is of a higher social status will answer ''yes'' to a question just to please the speaker.

It is possible to avoid the problems that can arise from such attitudes. Instead of asking a question that can be answered with ''yes'' or ''no,'' take a more controlled approach:

NOT: Is (name of town) near here?
BUT: How long will it take to get to (name of town)?

NOT: Will you be here tomorrow?
BUT: When will you come again?

In some places, in order to be kind to you, people will tell you what they think you want to hear in respect to when something will be accomplished. You may be told that shoes will be fixed right away, the dry cleaning will be done by tomorrow, and the car will be repaired by four o'clock.

In some places, some farewells are used and plans for future meetings are proposed that should not be taken literally unless the person making the remark offers or is asked about specific details. **Te veo mañana** (I will see you tomorrow) can mean only ''I would enjoy seeing you again.'' **Cenemos juntos el sábado** (Let's eat dinner together on Saturday) could indicate simply that the speaker thinks it would be very nice to get together some time.

❈

20. DISCUSSIONS

In any country, culture, or situation, common sense and the knowledge of the language and the culture should dictate the suitability of intervening in a discussion of certain issues, such as issues important by their nature (religion, politics, and world affairs) and issues important to the individual (sports, bullfighting, and where one is from). These topics should be handled with great care in Hispanic encounters, since feelings can run very deep, and reactions can be explosive.

Politics is a very common topic of conversation, and discussions of this subject can be very heated. Hispanics may talk very strongly against their government, their institutions, and even their own country, but it is prudent for a foreigner not even to show agreement with any such criticism. The Hispanic, in all probability, would take offense, construing this as an affront to his or her country.

❁

21. *DON, DOÑA*

The words **don** (used in addressing a man) and **doña** (used in addressing a woman) are untranslatable titles of respect. **Don** comes from the masculine Latin noun *dominus* (master of a house, head of a household, lord, master); **doña,** the feminine counterpart of **don,** comes from the feminine Latin noun *domina* (mistress of a house, lady). In the very distant past, **don** and **doña** were titles used for only a very few. Later, they came to be used for members of the nobility. At present, they are commonly used.

Don and **doña** are written in lower case in the middle of a sentence unless they are abbreviated. The abbreviations for **don** (**Dn.** or **D.**) and **doña** (**Dña.** or **D.ª**) are always capitalized: **Don Pedro** or **don Pedro** or **Dn. Pedro; Doña María** or **doña María** or **Dña. María.**

35

Don and **doña** are used:

only when immediately followed by the person's first name. The last name may or may not be added:

Don Juan está aquí.	Don Juan is here.
Don Juan García está aquí.	Don Juan Garcia is here.

with the person's first name, without the last name, to show respect and closeness when addressing or speaking of a person:

¿Cómo está, don Juan?
How are you, don Juan?

Doña Juana, ¿cómo está su esposo?
Doña Juana, how is your husband?

with older people with whom **señor** or **señora** followed by a last name would be too formal or too distant. You might call an elderly neighbor **doña Ana;** good family friends who are your parents' peers would be addressed as **don Pedro** and **doña Ana.**

with adults of about the same age as the speaker, but of much higher rank in business or social status, such as employees greeting or referring to the boss: **don Pedro** or **doña Ana;** and students referring to or greeting the teacher: **don Pedro** or **doña Ana.**

Don and **doña** are used in combination with the appropriate form of **señor** or **señora** in addressing a letter:

Sr. Dn. Pedro García   Sra. Dña. Ana Mendoza

While **don** can be used in addressing or referring to any male, single or married, the use of **doña** is restricted to married or widowed women only. The one exception is royalty, in which case **doña** can be used with the name of an unmarried woman:

la princesa doña Isabel   Princess doña Isabel

For any single woman, regardless of age, the parallel to **doña** before a first name is **señorita.** (See Point 55, ''**Señor, señora, señorita.**'')

✵

22. DRESS CODE

Hispanics of all ages and social situations usually give great importance to and place great value on appearance. The important issue is not the cost of the clothing, but its appropriateness and look. This attitude stems not from a desire to show off, but from an inherent sense of honor, dignity, and pride.

This does not mean that Hispanics do not like tennis shoes and blue jeans when they are appropriate.

Anyone who wishes to make a good impression in business or in social situations, or to avoid standing out as a foreigner, should be aware of the Hispanic outlook on dress. This might be especially valuable in places and situations where foreigners could be targets for pickpockets or others who take advantage of foreign tourists who appear not to be "in the know."

The use of black and other dark colors in clothing is much more prevalent in the Hispanic world than in our culture. This is due in great part to the use of black and eventually of somewhat lighter colors for mourning, which is often observed for an extended period. Women who are widowed may never again wear anything other than black, or black skirts or suits with white blouses. (See Point 16, "Conventionalism.")

In spite of the general formality in dress in the Hispanic world, in hot climates or during the hot season in other climates, men at work in offices often wear a **guayabera** (a light shirt) instead of the more formal dress shirt, tie, and coat. (A **guayabera** is a lightweight, loose-fitting, open-necked shirt that is cut straight across the bottom and is worn outside of the trousers. It typically has patch pockets, including one on either side of the front near the bottom, may have buttons near or on each side seam near the hem, and frequently has groups of small vertical tucks stitched from top to bottom. Dressier versions may have embroidered designs instead of tucks.)

Many places in the Hispanic world have regional costumes, which are usually colorful and elaborate. These often are worn by members of organizations who are taking part in festivals or other special celebrations.

❁

23. EDUCATION

Note that **educación** and related words very often refer to upbringing rather than to formal education: **Una persona bien educada** commonly means a well-mannered, well-brought-up person.

Education is often referred to as **enseñanza,** although many countries have a Department of Education called **Ministerio de Educación.** The educational system in the Hispanic world differs from that in the U.S. and, in varying degrees, from country to country.

Classroom activity is more structured, there is generally less student participation in class than there can be in our system. There are few extracurricular activities. The subjects taught are limited in scope to ''academic'' subjects, per se. On the pre-university level, there are schools where all courses are taught in a foreign language (in English, French, or German, for example), or where half of the subjects are taught in Spanish and half in a foreign language.

Pre-university level

There are many private schools, the majority of which are operated by the Church. Not many schools at this level are co-educational. In most schools students wear uniforms, if not always, at least on some occasions. The ''uniform'' may consist of only a light outer garment, like a lab coat.

The **escuela primaria** (or **escuela** or **colegio**) usually lasts six years; the **escuela secundaria** (or **colegio, instituto, academia,** or **liceo**) usually lasts six years as well.

Upon completion of high school, the **bachillerato** students receive the degree of **bachiller.** In some places, the degree is awarded only upon the passing of a comprehensive oral examination.

Both students and teachers are more interested in and actively involved in politics than is common in our culture. Sometimes, due to the general political situation or because of the political activity of the students, the **Ministerio de Educación** orders all high schools closed. In some cases, final exams have been moved forward or even canceled, the school year declared over, and students automatically promoted to the next level.

Both high school and university level

Most classes are large, and courses are taught predominantly by lecture. Usually the school year is a single unit of nine months (not divided into quarters or semesters), and exams include the material studied over the whole school year. Oral as well as written exams are given, and students are not always tested by the teacher who taught them. Grades are based on a numerical scale, such as 1 through 10.

University level

University-level studies offer highly structured programs to prepare students for a degree **(título)** in fields such as medicine, law, humanities, and science. Few (or no) electives are offered. Students must decide upon a career fairly early. In our culture, in casual conversation with youngsters, a typical question is what they are going to be when they grow up. In the Hispanic world, the question on this topic often is **"¿Qué carrera vas a estudiar?"** ("What career are you going to study?").

Very few **universidades** have a sprawling, lawn-covered campus **(ciudad universitaria** or **"campus")**; most consist of a single building or of a few buildings clustered together or scattered throughout the city. The equivalent of the university division we call a college is **Facultad,** or for technical fields, mainly in Spain, **Escuela, Escuela Especial,** or **Escuela Técnica Superior:**

> **Facultad de Filosofía y Letras**
> College of Philosophy and Letters (Liberal Arts)
>
> **Facultad de Medicina**
> College of Medicine
>
> **Escuela (Especial) de Ingenieros Aeronáuticos**
> School of Aeronautical Engineers
>
> **Escuela de Minas**
> School of Mines

People who graduate in different fields receive different degrees. **Licenciado** is the degree in the fields of arts and sciences; **ingeniero** is the degree in engineering; **arquitecto** is the architecture degree. The

39

parallel to the master's degree, where such is given, is **maestría;** the parallel to an M.D. or Ph.D. is **doctorado.** With the exception of **maestría,** all of the above degrees can be used as titles before a person's name:

licenciado Juan García	licenciada Juana García
ingeniero Miguel Mendoza	ingeniera María Mendoza
doctor Jaime Pérez	doctora Elena Pérez

There usually are no university-sponsored student residence halls; residences, if any, belong to private institutions. Students usually live in **pensiones** (boardinghouses) or private homes. Generally, there are no university-sponsored or related social organizations, activities, or sports. Participants in sports join clubs dedicated to a given sport. Most universities are autonomous, with no external governing board and little direct government involvement. They decide their own policies and teaching staff.

Universities are major centers of political activity. There are often politically motivated student strikes, with violent demonstrations; government troops may be called in to quell them. At times, a government closes a university because of antigovernment activity. If this is prolonged, it postpones graduation for the students.

Special programs

Many universities in the Hispanic world have programs, especially during our summer months, for foreign students. These programs are designed for students interested primarily in studying the Spanish language and Hispanic culture and literature.

✿

24. EXPRESSIONS SUCH AS ¡DIOS MÍO!

Expressions using **Dios, Jesús, María,** and the names of saints are heard frequently and are totally acceptable in Spanish. Some examples are:**¡Dios mío!** (My God!), **¡Válgame Dios!** (God help me!), **¡Por Dios!** (For God's sake!), **¡Jesús!** (said, for example, when someone sneezes), **¡María Santísima!** (Holy Mary!), **¡Que los ángeles benditos me ayuden!** (May the holy angels help me!).

With the exception of saying **¡Jesús!** when someone sneezes, it is advisable for a person not deeply immersed in Hispanic culture to avoid using such expressions. They would probably sound strange, artificial, and hollow.

❁

25. EYE CONTACT IN CONVERSATION

It is a sign of sincerity to maintain eye contact in conversation, but in some situations, such as facing superiors, parents, and teachers, lowering the eyes shows respect, not lack of it or guilt.

❁

26. FAMILY AND FRIENDS

The term **familia** usually means the extended family, not the nuclear family we think of in our culture. The extended family is the most important social unit in Hispanic culture, and may consist of father, mother, younger children, older children and their spouses and children, grandparents, aunts, uncles, and cousins, and in an outer circle, **padrinos** and **compadres.** (See Point 46, "**Padrino, madrina.**")

Family ties are very strong. Families are very open in their daily lives and people easily welcome friends of family members into their homes and at family gatherings. When someone travels or goes to another town or city to study or for a shorter stay, as for medical treatment, for instance, common practice is for that person to stay with relatives or even with friends of relatives. Many members of a family may live together in one household for cultural, practical, and economic reasons. The family is the shelter for young members, even married ones, until they are economically established. This is not considered lack of independence on the part of the young people or an imposition on the others. The family is also the refuge for the older members.

41

With changing economic and social conditions, the nuclear family is a growing phenomenon. This is seen particularly as young people leave home to find work in large cities.

Serving as a credit reference or as a personal reference is an important social function of the family. (See Point 31, ''Introductions.'')

Amigo/amiga (friend) is used in Spanish in its most literal sense: a real friend. Other more accurate, appropriate descriptive words are also used, such as **conocido/conocida** (acquaintance), **compañero/ compañera** (companion), as in **compañero de clase** (classmate) and **compañera de trabajo** (co-worker).

�֍

27. FORMS OF GOVERNMENT OR POLITICAL STATUS

The following are terms used in the descriptions of the forms of government of the countries of the Hispanic world.

Asamblea Legislativa	Legislative Assembly
Asamblea Nacional del Poder del Pueblo	National Assembly of the People's Power
Cámara de Diputados	Chamber of Deputies
Cámara de Representantes del Pueblo	House of Representatives of the People
Cámara de Senadores	Chamber of Senators
Congreso de Diputados	Congress of Deputies
Congreso Nacional	National Congress
Monarquía constitucional	Constitutional Monarchy (a titular monarch reigns; elected officials participate in the governing)
República federal	Federal Republic (power is divided between the central government and states, provinces, regions, etc.)
República unitaria	Unitary Republic (power is held by a central authority, not derived from nor shared with administrative subdivisions)
Senado	Senate

Description of the Forms of Government of the Countries of the Hispanic World:

Argentina	Federal republic, two legislative houses: **Senado** (46 members), **Cámara de Diputados** (254 members)
Bolivia	Unitary multiparty republic, two legislative houses: **Cámara de Senadores** (27 members), **Cámara de Diputados** (130 members)
Colombia	Unitary multiparty republic, two legislative houses: **Senado** (144 members), **Cámara de Representantes** (199 members)
Costa Rica	Unitary multiparty republic, one legislative house: **Asamblea Legislativa** (57 members)
Cuba	Unitary socialist republic, one legislative house: **Asamblea Nacional del Poder del Pueblo** (150 members)
Chile	Unitary republic, two legislative houses; **Senado** (47 members), **Cámara de diputados** (120 members)
Ecuador	Unitary multiparty republic, one legislative house: **Congreso Nacional** (71 members)
El Salvador	Republic, one legislative house: **Asamblea Legislativa** (60 members)
España	Constitutional monarchy, two legislative houses: **Senado** (257 members), **Congreso de Diputados** (350 members), chief of state: the king; head of government: the prime minister
Guatemala	Republic, one legislative house: **Congreso de la República** (100 members)
Guinea Ecuatorial	Unitary single-party republic, one legislative house: **Cámara de Representantes del Pueblo** (41 members)
Honduras	Multiparty republic, one legislative house: **Congreso** (134 members)
México	Federal republic, two legislative houses: **Senado** (64 members), **Cámara de Diputados** (500 members)
Nicaragua	Unitary multiparty republic, one legislative house: **Asamblea Nacional** (96 members)
Panamá	Multiparty republic, one legislative house: **Asamblea Legislativa** (67 members)
Paraguay	Republic, two legislative houses: **Senado** (30 members), **Cámara de Diputados** (60 members)
Perú	Unitary multiparty republic, two legislative houses: **Senado** (60 members), **Cámara de Diputados** (180 members)

Puerto Rico	Self-governing commonwealth associated with the U.S.; two legislative houses: **Senado** (27 members), **Cámara de Representantes** (51 members), chief of state: president of the U.S.; head of government: the governor
República Dominicana	Multiparty republic, two legislative houses: **Senado** (30 members), **Cámara de Diputados** (120 members)
Uruguay	Republic, two legislative houses: **Senado** (31 members), **Cámara de Representantes** (99 members)
Venezuela	Federal multiparty republic, two legislative houses: **Senado** (47 members), **Cámara de Diputados** (200 members)

28. GESTURES

Gestures tend to be used more in Spanish-speaking countries than in ours. Since different countries have different gestures, or may have the same gesture with different meanings, with rare exceptions, non-natives should avoid using them.

People often think that voids in knowledge of language can be filled with hand signals and gestures, but this can be socially hazardous. Gestures can have crude or less-than-polite meanings, and an innocent gesture from one's home country can be all wrong in another place. In general, don't imitate gestures. A gesture you witness and understand may be acceptable in the ''hands'' of some but not in those of others, or even in those of the same people in different situations. Therefore, even though you may understand a gesture, it is best not to imitate it.

Be sure to know just who can use a certain gesture, and when it is appropriate. Reserve any new appropriate gesture for use only in the country where you learned it, or in the country of the person from whom you learned it, and only at the social level in which you learned it, until you know otherwise.

Standard, "safe" gestures

The gestures described below are universally understood throughout the Hispanic world and may be used safely.

come here: hold forearm up, palm away from you and slightly inclined, move the fingers down, then up, repeating the motion.

good-bye: hold forearm up, palm facing you, move the fingers toward you, then away, repeating the motion rapidly.

so-so: hold palm facing downward, fingers spread, elbow close to your side; shrug shoulders; lean head to the side of the hand used for the gesture; tip hand from side to side fairly rapidly.

be careful: place tip of index finger under the center of the eye and pull slightly downward.

to indicate that someone is stingy: bend forearm upward, close to the body; with cupped palm of the other hand, lightly tap the bent elbow.

to indicate a person's height: in some places, the palm is held facing sideways, since the palm facing down is used to measure height of animals.

to indicate excellence: put the tips of all five fingers together, kiss them, then instantly move the hand straight ahead and spread the fingers. This gesture is applicable to anything, and is commonly used to indicate the quality of food.

to send a kiss as a gesture of farewell: kiss the fingertips on the palm side, as we do, then move the hand slightly away from the lips.

to indicate money: with palm facing upward and index and middle fingers together, rub the thumb over the tips of these two fingers.

to indicate a small amount, or "just a minute": hold the hand up in front of you, palm facing sideways. Curl the last three fingers toward the palm, extend the index finger and thumb parallel to each other, with an inch or less of space between them.

"**no**": with hand up, palm facing outward, thumb and second finger touching and index finger straight up, move hand at the wrist from side to side.

to indicate that you want to eat, to suggest eating, or to ask if it's time to eat: with hand up, fingers together, and palm toward the face, bend the fingers down; bring thumb up to touch the underside of the first three fingers; move the hand back and forth toward the mouth.

❁

29. GREETINGS AND SALUTATIONS

Of course the most common greetings are **Buenos días** (Good morning), **Buenas tardes** (Good afternoon), **Buenas noches** (Good evening), and **¡Hola!** (Hi!). These phrases may be used by people who greet each other in passing, or may be used as greetings before beginning a conversation. People who wish to greet or acknowledge others without stopping to chat may say **¡Adiós!** to one another. This is most often used by people who aren't close enough friends to stop and greet each other in a more substantial way, by those who are at too great a distance to greet one another in a different fashion, and by those who are in too much of a hurry to stop briefly and talk. It is used mainly in outdoor situations, such as when passing on the sidewalk or in traffic. In similar situations indoors, as in walking down a corridor or a supermarket aisle, one of the other common greetings would usually be used.

If a person is eating or is about to eat and wants to greet someone who sees him or her, a common salutation would be **¿Usted gusta?** or **¿Gustas?** or **¿Ustedes gustan?** (Would you like to join me? literally Do you like?).

The required answer in this case is **No, muchas gracias, ¡buen provecho!** or **No, muchas gracias, ¡que aproveche!** (No, thank you, enjoy your meal!), or another appropriate response: informally to one person: **No, muchas gracias, ¡que te aproveche!**; formally to one person: **No, muchas gracias, ¡que le aproveche!**; informally to more than one person: **No, muchas gracias, ¡que os aproveche!**; formally (in some places informally) to more than one person: **No muchas gracias, ¡que les aproveche!**

If you see someone eating or about to eat and want to greet him or her, you can say **¡Buen aprovecho!** or **¡Que aproveche!** (Enjoy your meal! Bon appetit!) or informally to one person: **¡Que te aproveche!**; formally to one person: **¡Que le aproveche!**; informally to more than one person: **¡Que os aproveche!**; formally (in some places informally) to more than one person: **¡Que les aproveche!**

The response to these salutations is always **Gracias** (Thank you) or **Muchas gracias** (Thank you very much).

Shaking hands, embracing, kissing

When people stop to greet one another, there will probably be some physical contact, as well as a verbal exchange. Friends and acquaintances (male and female, from teenage up) almost always shake hands when meeting and when parting. When a man and a woman shake hands, the man may slightly bow his head or his upper body. This gesture of politeness is a remnant of bowing to kiss a woman's hand.

Women often embrace and kiss on one or both cheeks. Often, only their cheeks touch; the kiss is more of a gesture than an actual kiss. Men and women may also embrace and kiss on the cheek, but only if they are relatives or very close friends.

Men often embrace (one arm under the shoulder of the other person, the other arm over the shoulder), especially if they haven't seen one another for a while or if they are saying good-bye when one is leaving to be gone for some time. They may also pat each other firmly once or twice on the back as they embrace.

Kissing

Women (from teenage up) frequently kiss or make the gesture of kissing on the cheek in hugs of greeting and farewell. Men and women (from teenage up) will do this only if they are relatives or very close friends. People never kiss on the lips, except in a romantic situation. Children and parents never kiss on the lips. Even a husband and wife saying good-bye would usually kiss on the cheek.

❖

30. HOUSING AND HOUSES

Although it is impossible to make generalizations about housing in the Hispanic world, some differences can be pointed out with regard to the usual structure and arrangement of single-family dwellings. Homes usually do not have a yard. The front door (and the door of the garage, if any) are flush with the street or with the sidewalk, which also usually has nothing between it and the street. Houses often share common walls with neighboring buildings. Enclosed patios are common. They vary in size and function; some are gardens, others are more utilitarian. In some countries, open ground areas, such as patios, are protected by high brick or adobe walls topped with good-size pieces of broken glass, usually from broken bottles. Many houses have a flat roof **(azotea),** where small living quarters for a maid, a laundry area, and a place for drying clothes might be found. Many houses have grillwork **(reja)** over the windows and as part of the structure of balconies on the upper floors.

In cities, buildings with offices or stores on the ground floor often have apartments above. These high-rise residences may have an opening to the sky—not a patio, but a way to provide light and air. The interior floors of many houses are of highly polished wood or glazed ceramic floor tiles (**baldosas** or the smaller, finer **baldosines**).

The walls of many kitchens are covered with glazed ceramic wall tiles (**azulejos**). These may be of a solid color or may have a geometric design or pattern; several together may form a larger pattern.

Since most houses are constructed with thick adobe, brick, or concrete walls that do not allow for built-in closets, people use pieces of furniture (**armarios, roperos**) to store clothing, linens, and so forth. In some homes, storage niches are made in the walls, or a closet called an **alacena** is made by walling off a corner of a room.

❖

31. INTRODUCTIONS

Because of the strength and importance of family ties, and of relative geographic stability, people are often introduced and referred to in relationship to their connection with a known or prominent member of their family (see Point 26, ''Family and friends.''):

> **Le presento a Carlos, el hijo de don Enrique Valbuena.**
> May I introduce Carlos, don Enrique Valbuena's son.

In introducing a female friend, a man (especially a married man) should refer to her as **una amiga mía,** not as **mi amiga.** This is due to one of the possible meanings of **amiga** (paramour), and the exclusivity that **mi** expresses. By the same token, a woman (again, especially a married woman) should refer to a male friend as **un amigo mío**.

32. KITCHEN

When visiting in someone's home, do not be too friendly with the household help. This could be viewed as undermining the authority of the woman of the house. (See Point 39, ''Maids.'')

Never go into the kitchen unless invited. It is the domain of the household help and the woman of the house.

A man should never offer to help in the kitchen, or even to help clear the table. These tasks are looked upon as women's work, and a man seen doing them is usually greatly frowned upon.

33. LAWS AND REGULATIONS

Generally speaking, Hispanics are not characterized by blind acceptance of or submission to authority or control. Laws and regulations are not considered absolutes; there is always room for interpretation or rationalization.

34. LEFT-HANDED PEOPLE

In some places, especially less acculturated ones, left-handed people (**zurdos**) attract attention in a negative way. They may be viewed somewhat suspiciously and as bearers of bad luck. Such attitudes are holdovers from folklore and superstitious belief.

35. LEGAL CODE

Anyone who encounters trouble with the law should be aware that in Hispanic countries, the Napoleonic Code rules: a person is guilty until proven innocent. There is no such thing as plea bargaining, and trials are not by jury.

36. LETTERS, GREETING CARDS, AND ANNOUNCEMENTS

All mail to Hispanic countries should be sent by air mail. Other methods of delivery can take months.

Generally speaking, Hispanics do not write letters with the same frequency that we do.

Personal letters

Personal letters tend to be somewhat formal, respectful in tone, and complicated in style.

Salutation

For family and very close friends:

Querido . . . :, Querida . . . :,	Dear . . . ,
Queridos . . . :, Queridas . . . :	
Querido amigo/Querida amiga . . . :,	Dear friend . . . ,
etc.	

Note that a colon is used in Spanish, instead of a comma.

For other acquaintances and friends, "Dear . . . ," is written:

Estimado . . . :, Estimada . . . :, etc.	Esteemed . . . ,
Estimado amigo/Estimada amiga	Esteemed friend . . . ,
. . . :, etc.	
Apreciado . . . :, Apreciada . . . :,	Appreciated . . . ,
etc.	
Apreciado amigo/Apreciada amiga	Appreciated friend . . . ,
. . . :, etc.	

When the letter is for a couple or a family, the man's name comes first in the salutation:

Queridos Martín y María:	Dear Martin and Maria,
Queridos Martín, María y Pedrito:	Dear Martin, Maria, and Pedrito,

Body of personal letters

Paragraphs are usually indented to the length of the salutation. Most letters open with a fairly formal, routine, but sincere introductory paragraph, such as:

Querida María:

  Espero que al recibo de ésta tú y los tuyos os encontréis bien de salud como nosotros os deseamos. Aquí, a Dios gracias, todos lo estamos.

Dear Maria,

  I hope that on receipt of this you and yours are well, the way we wish for you. Here, thanks to God, we are all fine.

The body of most letters is generally less informative and less detailed than ours.

> **Acabamos de mudarnos de casa. A los niños les gusta la escuela. José sigue jugando en el equipo de fútbol de su colegio.**
>
> We have just moved. The children like school. Jose is continuing to play on his high school soccer team.

Closing of personal letters

The closing is similar to the introduction in formality and length. Here, the writer sends additional greetings, concluding with a sentence of farewell, which ends with a comma that leads to the closing and signature.

> **Os mandamos nuestros saludos a todos.**
> (a man might continue:)
> **Recibe un fuerte abrazo de tu hermano que te quiere,**
> > **(firma)**
>
> We send our greetings to all of you. Receive a big hug from your brother who loves you,
> > (signature)
>
> (a woman might continue:)
> **Con mucho cariño y muchos besos se despide tu hermana que mucho te quiere,**
> > **(firma)**
>
> With much love and many kisses, your sister who loves you a lot says good-bye,
> > (signature)

Following are examples of very informal closings:

Besos	Kisses
Abrazos	Hugs
Un fuerte abrazo	A big hug

Business and other formal letters

Business letters and similar correspondence tend to be relatively florid and complimentary.

Beginning of business and other formal letters

These letters begin with the date, but they rarely include the address of the sender.

With or without a complete inside address, the name of the person to whom the letter is written is given.

Sr. Dn.	or	**Reverendo Padre**	or	**Excmo. Sr. Dn.**
Alonso González		**Juan Pérez**		**Mariano Grau**

(**Excmo. Sr.** is the abbreviation of **Excelentísimo señor.**)

After a couple of spaces will be the greeting, which does not usually include the person's name. For example:

Muy señor mío:	Dear Sir:
Muy señora mía:	Dear Madam:
Distinguida señora:	Madam:
Distinguidos señores:	Gentlemen:

With the person's name, the greeting can be as follows:

Estimado Sr. González:

If the addressee has a title, it is repeated, with or without the last name. In this case, however, the title is not preceded by a term such as **Estimado.**

Reverendo Padre: or   **Reverendo Padre Pérez:**

The greeting is followed by a colon.

Body of business and other formal letters

Paragraphs are indented to the length of the salutation, unlike the style in the U.S. in which the first line is often not indented.

Examples of introductory sentences in a business letter:

Sr. Dn.
Alonso González
Muy señor mío:
        Tenemos el gusto de remitir su pedido del 24 de septiembre.
    We have the pleasure of sending your order of September 24.
or
        En conformidad con la petición contenida en su atenta del 18 de mayo . . .
    According to the request contained in your kind (letter) of May 18 . . .

Closing of business and other formal letters

Business letters close with a short farewell sentence that usually does not end with a period, but is completed in sense by the phrase that follows it. This phrase may be one of several that are equivalents of "Sincerely yours," "Yours truly," and the like. It is written toward the right.

    Aprovechamos la ocasión para afirmarnos de Ud.
    We take the opportunity to affirm ourselves as your
        Attos. SS. SS.,
        Attentive, reliable servants

        (signature)

        (typed name)

(**Attos.** stands for **atentos** [attentive]; **SS. SS.** stands for **seguros servidores** [reliable servants]. See Point 1, "Abbreviations and acronyms.")
Nos despedimos de Uds.
We say good-bye to you
        Muy atentamente,
        Very attentively,

or

Esperando su contestación, quedo de Ud.
Waiting for your answer, I remain your

Atto. y S.S.,
Attentive and reliable servant,

One may conclude simply with a complete sentence and add a closing such as **Atentamente** (Sincerely).

Addresses (See Point 61, "Street names and addresses.")

Envelopes

In some places it is very common for individuals to use a post office box (**apartado de correos** or **casilla postal**) instead of having mail delivered to a street address. Note that **apartado** may be abbreviated (**Apdo.**); **casilla** may not.

Sr. Dn.	or	**Sr. Dn.**
Juan García		**Juan García**
Apdo. 318		**Casilla 318**
San José, Costa Rica		**La Paz, Bolivia**

A postal zone number may precede the name of the city:

28036 Madrid   **C.P. 40440**   (**código postal,** postal code)
México, D.F.

Divisions within cities can have a neighborhood name instead of, or in addition to, a postal zone number. This name should be included in the address. In Mexico, these divisions are called **colonias,** in Guatemala, they are **zonas,** in Chile they are **poblaciones.** In other places, the word **barrio** or **barriada** may be used.

The name of the addressee, in either a personal or a business letter, is most politely written with titles, which are abbreviated, and in this format:

Sr. Dn.	or	**Srtas.**
Juan García		**Elena y Rosa García**

Sometimes, mainly in sprawling cities, you can find more detailed addresses, which are further complicated by lack of standardization for them, and by the lack of rules about abbreviations in Spanish.

A residential address in Mexico City might look like this:

Mario Pereda	the person's name
Calle: Juan Gutiérrez	**Calle** (Street)
Lote: 23. Manzana 40	**Lote** (Lot); **Manzana** (Block)
Colonia: Guadalupe del Moral	**Colonia** (Colony) (Mexico City is divided into large areas called **colonias,** each with its own name.)
C.P. 40440	**C.P. (código postal,** postal code)
México, D.F.	**D.F. (Distrito Federal,**[3] Federal District) (**D.F.** parallels our Washington, D.C.)

The same address might also be written this way:

Mario Pereda
C.: Juan Gutiérrez
Lte.: 23. Ma.: 40
Col: Gpe. del Moral
C.P. 40440
México, D.F.
México

If the letter is sent to an entire family, even if it is a woman writing to her sister and family, the envelope is usually addressed to the male head of the family, with **y familia** following his name, on the same line:

Sr. Dn.
Juan García y familia
(address)

---

[3]Mexico, Venezuela, and Argentina have a Federal District.

A letter to a husband and wife would be addressed:

Sr. Dn.	or	**Sres.**
Juan García y señora		**Dn. Juan García**
(address)		**Dña. Mariquita Pérez**
		(address)

The return address usually appears on the back of the envelope, at the top and center of the closed flap. It is introduced with **Rmte:**, which is the abbreviation of **Remitente** (sender) or **Remite,** a verb form meaning that the one whose name follows ''is sending.''

Rmte: Ana Ortiz
(address)

Greeting cards

People in the Hispanic world do not usually send as many greeting cards for occasions and events as we do. Christmas cards are not sent in the quantities that they are in the U.S. Birthday cards are becoming more prevalent.

Announcements

Announcement cards, which are usually sent to announce a wedding or a death, are more common than greeting cards.

37. LOCALISMS, REGIONALISMS, AND NATIONALISMS

Due to the geographical extension and topographical diversity of the Hispanic world, the relative isolation of its many parts, and the varied linguistic influences that have come to bear on the Spanish language, it is to be expected that there will be localisms, regionalisms, and nationalisms. Learning localisms, especially in individual vocabulary words, can result in using words that cannot be (or are not usually) used in other parts of the Spanish-speaking world. For instance, the standard word for *bus* is **autobús** or **ómnibus,** but in Mexico *bus* is **camión** (which elsewhere means *truck);* in Bolivia, it is **góndola;** in Cuba, it is **guagua** (in Bolivia, this means *a tiny baby,* from the Quechua **wawa**).

Taxi in Mexico can be **libre** (free), apparently from the sign **"Libre,"** which is displayed when the taxi is available, and/or from the question ¿**Libre?** ("[Are you] free?").

Suitcase can be **maleta** in Spain, **petaca** in Mexico, and **valija** in Ecuador; *ticket* can be **billete** in Spain, **boleto** in Bolivia, and **tique** or **tiquete** in Colombia.

Using localisms from one place in another country can produce misunderstanding and perhaps even embarrassment. (See Point 72, "Words with multiple meanings.") You will usually be understood if you use standard terms.

❏

38. *LOS ESTADOS UNIDOS* AND THE TERM "AMERICAN"

There are several different ways a person from the United States can be designated. One term is **estadounidense,** a word based on the phrase **estados unidos.** While there are other countries in the Western Hemisphere besides the U.S.A. **(Estados Unidos de América)** with this phrase in their names **(Estados Unidos Mexicanos, Estados Unidos de Venezuela,** and **Estados Unidos del Brasil),** the term

estadounidense specifically designates someone from the United States of America. In Spanish America, it is important for a person from the U.S.A. not to refer to himself or herself as an "American," because all peoples of North, Central, and South America are Americans. He or she may be addressed or referred to with that term (**americano** for a male; **americana** for a female). Nevertheless, it may be considered presumptuous on the part of someone from the U.S. to initiate its use. The term for *North American* (**norteamericano** for a male; **norteamericana** for a female) is appropriate for someone from the U.S. Canadians are **canadienses;** Mexicans are **mexicanos** or **mejicanos.** In Spain, people from the U.S. are referred to as "Americans" (**americanos/americanas**) to the extent that if you use the term **norteamericano** or **estadounidense** people may react with a quizzical look.

❁

39. MAIDS

It is very common for Hispanic families of the middle and upper classes to have a **criada** (maid). The **criada** often lives in, and helps the woman of the house with, or is in charge of, any and all household chores, from grocery shopping and meal preparation and serving to caring for the children and answering the phone. A **criada** may be with the family for a long time, and is often considered practically a member of the family.

A guest in a home with a **criada** usually should not ask the maid directly to do things for him or her, but should ask the **señora** instead. Guests should not be too friendly toward maids or other household help; this could be taken as undermining the authority of the people of the house.

The terms for *maid* vary. They range from those that are generally understood throughout the Hispanic world, such as **criada** (maid), **sirvienta** (maid, servant), **muchacha (de servir)** or **muchacha (de servicio)** (serving girl), and **chica** (girl) to those that are more regional in usage, such as the following, which mean *servant:* **mucama** (in Argentina, Chile, Peru, and Uruguay) and **china** or **chinita** (from the Quechua word **china** [female]).

❁

40. MEALS AND MEALTIMES

Hispanics usually have three meals and perhaps a **merienda** (see ''Late afternoon'' below).

Early morning: *desayuno* (breakfast)

Breakfast, of course, is eaten at the time of the morning most appropriate for the individual. It is never the heavy meal that we might have in the U.S. It usually consists of a continental breakfast: coffee, milk (hot or cold), or **café con leche** (coffee with milk), and bread or rolls with butter or marmalade. Note that **café con leche** is not coffee with just a few drops of cream or milk (which is called a **cortado**), but is usually half coffee and half milk, to which sugar is ordinarily added.

Late morning: *tomar las once* (literally, "to take the eleven")

This is the least common of all meals. This idiomatic phrase is used in speaking of having a light snack between breakfast and the midday meal. In Colombia, it is used in reference to having a **merienda** (see below). **Tomar las onces** is also used euphemistically by men to refer to having some **aguardiente,** a distilled alcoholic drink whose name contains eleven letters.

Midday: *comida* (dinner, the main meal of the day) or *almuerzo* (lunch)

The meal at midday is usually eaten between one and three o'clock, and most people come home from work or school at that time. At least one and a half to two hours is reserved for this mealtime, after which people return to work or school. This does not mean that all this time is spent at the table: people may rest after the meal; male adults may go to a cafe or to a **tertulia** for a short while. (See Point 63, ''**Tertulia.**'')

Late afternoon: *merienda* or in some places *té* (small snack, similar to English tea)

The **merienda,** which consists of a small snack of sandwiches and pastries and something to drink, is had at some time around five or six o'clock. It is often very informal, and may be just for children.

Evening: *cena* (supper, dinner)

The evening meal is sometimes as late as nine, ten, or even eleven o'clock, especially in Spain. In some places, the **merienda** is skipped and the **cena** is served at an earlier hour.

If the midday meal was a **comida,** the **cena** is a lighter supper; if the midday meal was an **almuerzo,** the **cena** is a larger dinner. When Spanish speakers follow the meal pattern of our culture, **almuerzo** is eaten around noon. The later meal of the day is then referred to as either **comida** (dinner) or **cena** (supper).

Tapas (hors d'oeuvres)

Particularly in Spain, before dinner or supper people may have a before-dinner drink accompanied by **tapas** in a bar or **café.** This custom is more common among men than among women.

Tapas are small portions of foods suitable for nibbling, such as olives, almonds, sausage bits, cold cuts, assorted seafoods (anchovies, sardines, shrimp, clams, mussels, octopus, squid), a type of potato salad, potato chips, cheese, wedges of a **tortilla** (the term in Spain for omelet). (A **tortilla** is prepared in a small- to medium-size skillet. The omelet, which is firm and about an inch thick, is placed on a plate and cut in wedges. It can be served hot or cold. A **tortilla española** has pieces of sautéed potato in it.)

At times, people, especially foreign visitors, will make a meal of the numerous delicious **tapas** that are available, preferring these to a "real" meal.

Modern **tapas** have their origin in the old tavern custom of covering a slender wine or shot glass with a slice of hard sausage or ham (**una tapa**, from **tapar**, to cover), which was eaten as an accompaniment to the drink.

Midday and evening meals

These meals are important family or social events. They are eaten slowly; people relax and enjoy their food and the conversation. Especially when guests are present, the meal may be followed by the **sobremesa**, a time to linger and talk over coffee and perhaps an after-dinner drink.

It should be noted that after-dinner drinks are usually served only to the men; if both men and women are served, a stronger drink, such as brandy, is usually offered to the men and a liqueur is served to the women.

As we might invite people to our homes for dessert, Hispanics invite people for a **sobremesa**, which probably would include dessert.

Notes on dinner and supper

Dessert is most often fruit, served sometimes with cheese. A very popular dessert is **flan**, baked custard with a caramel topping. If a dessert such as **flan**, ice cream, or pastry is served, it does not replace the fruit dessert; it is served after the fruit. When fruit, other than grapes or cherries, is served, it is peeled and eaten at the table with a knife and fork.

Wine is the customary beverage at dinner and supper. Children may also be served wine, diluted with water or a citrus-based soft drink. It should be noted that alcohol consumption is not regulated by law in the Hispanic world.

Coffee is not usually drunk with dinner or supper, but after the meal, and is much stronger than that ordinarily served in the U.S. Generally it is espresso or cappuccino, served in a demitasse.

Eating in restaurants

People in our culture may tend to be friendly to waiters and waitresses in restaurants, at times chatting briefly with them. This is not customary in Hispanic culture.

If you are at a table, and friends or acquaintances pass by, they may greet you by saying **¡Buen provecho!** (Bon appetit! Enjoy your meal!). (See Point 29, ''Greetings and salutations.'')

Eating in a public place other than a restaurant

People eating in a public place (on a train or a bus, for example) may, as a gesture of courtesy, offer something to people nearby, saying **¿Ud. gusta?** or **¿Uds. gustan?** (Would you like some?). The appropriate response is **No, gracias. ¡Que aproveche!** or **No, gracias. ¡Buen provecho!** (No, thanks. Enjoy your meal!).

Similarly, cigarettes or candy may be offered, in which case one could accept. If declining the offer, one says **No, muchas gracias.**

❁

41. MILESTONES

There are several milestones in life that are observed in some way or another in different cultures and societies. In the Hispanic world, although observances may vary, as they do in our own culture, there is general recognition of birth, birthdays, graduations, weddings, wedding anniversaries, and death.

Baptisms and especially first communions are also important milestones, and are marked by large celebrations. In some places, especially Spain, the celebration of the first communion, which a child usually takes around the age of nine, has become an elaborate (and at times expensive) event, with the child receiving many gifts.

63

In some places in the Hispanic world, especially in Mexico, in Central America, and in the Caribbean, a girl's fifteenth birthday is an event for celebration, since it indicates that she has come of age, and is now a woman. The girl, **la quinceañera** (from **quince,** fifteen, and **año,** year), is feted at a **fiesta de los quince años,** which can be a very elaborate affair.

A boy's coming of age is recognized when he turns twenty-one. Generally speaking, birthdays are not really celebrated as they usually are in our culture; a person's saint's day is given greater emphasis. (See Point 47, ''People's names.'') However, in some places, perhaps due to influence from our country, birthdays are special, festive occasions.

When someone dies, it is not uncommon for the family to send an **esquela de defunción** or **esquela mortuoria,** a formal, printed schematic announcement of the death. Also, unlike the usual obituary notice that appears in our newspapers, telling something about the life of the deceased and sometimes even the cause of death, it is more common in the Hispanic world to print a duplicate of the **esquela de defunción.**

In some places, in observance of the anniversary of someone's death, it is common to have a mass said. The announcement of the mass appears in the newspaper in a rather large, often multicolumn box, framed in black, and is similar to the **esquela de defunción.** It may indicate by whom the mass is offered, which could be family members, friends, or even the company for which the person had worked.

42. MONETARY UNITS AND THEIR SYMBOLS

| Country | Monetary unit | | 1/100 |
	name	symbol	
Argentina	peso	$	centavo
Bolivia	peso	Bs	centavo
Chile	peso	Ch$	centavo
Colombia	peso	Col$	centavo
Costa Rica	colón	₡	céntimo
Cuba	peso	CUP	centavo
Dominican Republic	peso	RD$	centavo
Ecuador	sucre	S/.	centavo
El Salvador	colón	₡	centavo
Equatorial Guinea	franc	CFAF	centime
Guatemala	quetzal	Q	centavo
Honduras	lempira	L	centavo
Mexico	peso	Mex$	centavo
Nicaragua	córdoba	C$	centavo
Panama	balboa	B	centésimo
Paraguay	guaraní	₲	céntimo
Peru	inti[1]	I/.	céntimo
Spain	peseta	Pta.	céntimo
Uruguay	peso	NUr$	centésimo
Venezuela	bolívar	B	céntimo

Puerto Rico, officially **Estado Libre Asociado de Puerto Rico** (the Commonwealth of Puerto Rico), has the U.S. dollar as its monetary unit.

Mexico often uses **MN (moneda nacional,** national currency) following a price.

Note: Except for **peseta** and **lempira,** all of the monetary units given above, including **córdoba** and **balboa,** are masculine in gender.

[1]Prior to 1985, the unit of currency of Peru was the **sol** (sun). **Inti,** the name of the current monetary unit, is the Quechua word for *sun.*

❁

43. NAVIGATING A BUILDING

Labeling/numbering of floors

Piso means *floor, story.* The ground floor is the **planta baja (P.B.)** or the **piso bajo** (also **P.B.**). The next floor is the **primer piso** (first floor, first story). The next floor is the **segundo piso** (second floor, second story). In some places, such as large cities in Spain, one may find the following:

planta baja	ground floor
entresuelo	mezzanine
principal	another mezzanine
primero	fourth floor
segundo	fifth floor

In apartment buildings, the lowest floors are considered the choice locations, unless, of course, there is a desirable view or some other factor that makes a higher level more appealing.

An elevator may have these symbols:

0	**(cero)** for the basement, which could be the garage level
B or **P.B.**	for **planta baja** or **piso bajo** the ground floor
1	
2	
etc.	

❂

44. NOISE

Apparently, the tolerance level for noise is higher in the Hispanic world than in our country. In conversation, loudness is generally not a sign of anger, but could merely be an indication of enthusiasm or a reinforcement of what is being said.

In public gathering places (cafes, game arcades, carnivals, and the like), the noise level can be extremely high according to our standards. In any social gathering, noise can be high, too.

❂

45. NUMBER USAGE IN DIFFERENT SITUATIONS

Numbers are not "broken" in Spanish. *1985* is never "nineteen eighty-five," but **mil novecientos ochenta y cinco** (one thousand nine hundred eighty-five). *267* Cleveland Drive is never "two six seven," but **doscientos sesenta y siete** (two hundred sixty-seven). *Classroom 305* is **el aula trescientos cinco.**

There are some exceptions to this rule:

The digits in hotel-room numbers may be grouped to indicate the floor and the room number: *2506* is **veinticinco cero seis.**

The digits in phone numbers sometimes are grouped, sometimes read as individual digits. If the digits are grouped in printing, they are read in those groups:

> **33-82-41** is **treinta y tres, ochenta y dos, cuarenta y uno.**

If the digits are not grouped by pairs, they may be read as separate digits or grouped:

> **241-0627** might be **dos, cuatro, uno, cero, seis, dos, siete**
> or, more likely:
> **doscientos cuarenta y uno, cero, seis, veintisiete.**

When you say a U.S. phone number in Spanish, one way is to give the three digits of the area code **(código territorial)** and the first three digits of the phone number **(número de teléfono)** individually, and then to group the last four digits:

> **(515) 294-4228**   **cinco uno cinco, dos nueve cuatro, cuarenta y dos, veintiocho**

A zip code **(código postal),** a credit-card number **(número de tarjeta dc crédito),** or any other large number is read the way that seems the easiest or best way to be understood.

The number *seven* is written with a line across the middle (7), so that it is not confused with the number *one,* which is written with a "lead" line (1), not simply as a straight line.

A comma is used where we normally use a decimal point, and a decimal point where we normally use a comma: **2,95; 2.005,98.**

When the word **o** (or) is used between numbers, especially when handwritten, it has an accent on it (**ó**) to avoid its being confused with the number zero: **2 ó 3** (2 or 3).

Except for punctuation, one million/**un millón** is the same in both English and Spanish: 1,000,000 = **1.000.000.**

> 1,000,000,000 in English is one billion
> **1.000.000.000** in Spanish is **mil millones**
>
> 1,000,000,000,000 in English is one trillion
> **1.000.000.000.000** in Spanish is **un billón** or **un millón de millones**

❁

46. *PADRINO, MADRINA; COMPADRE, COMADRE*

When Hispanic children are baptized, their parents ask two people to be **padrinos** (godparents) to serve as religious sponsors. The **padrino** [godfather] and **madrina** [godmother] assume the responsibility for the child's being brought up in the faith and act as guardians in case of the death of the parents.

Children may acquire different **padrinos** for other sacraments, such as confirmation, marriage, and, in the case of men, ordination into the priesthood. However, the strongest ties between child and **padrinos** are those established with the godparents from baptism.

The **padrinos,** and especially the godfather, provide the **ahijado** (godson) or **ahijada** (goddaughter) with a second family. Godparents do not have to be married; if they are married, they need not be married to each other. The parents may seek godparents from among people of higher social status than themselves. The resulting ties between godparents and the child and the child's family could be beneficial, even providing a way to improve the social status of the parents, or at least of the child.

The relationship between the godparents (especially the god-father) and the child and the child's family goes beyond religious obligation. Until quite recently (November 1983), the Catholic Church forbade marriage between a godparent and his or her godchild. This attitude underlines the strength and character of the ties that are to be established and maintained between godparent and godchild.

With the new bond of **padrinazgo** (godparenthood) comes another new relationship, **compadrazgo,** between the godparents and the natural parents of the child. The father and the godfather call each other **compadre** (literally ''co-father'') and the mother and the **madrina** are **comadres.** (By extension, in some places, friends and acquaintances call each other **compadres.**)

✿

47. PEOPLE'S NAMES AND NAME DAYS

Full names

Traditionally, the **nombre completo** (full name) of a Hispanic consists of the **nombre de pila** (first name), followed by two surnames—the **apellido paterno** (father's family name) and the **apellido materno** (mother's family name), in that order.

In Spain, however, since 1984, it has been legal for adults to reverse the order of the last names, placing the mother's family name first and making that the principal family name. Since 1987, newborns can be named in the same way.

In Chile, since the publication of law Number 17,344 in 1970, people who have been known for five or more years by the same name may completely change any or all parts of their name, if they can show that they have one of the reasons acceptable by law to make the change. These reasons include having a strange-sounding or embarrassing name, being illegitimate, or changing sex.

First names

A person's first name is his or her **nombre de pila** (baptismal name; literally "name of baptismal font"). This is shortened to **nombre** on most forms.

It is customary to name the firstborn son in a family after his father or his godfather, **padrino de bautizo.** Less frequently, the firstborn daughter is given her mother's first name, or that of her godmother. (See Point 46, "**Padrino, madrina; compadre, comadre.**")

People of the highest social strata or of noble rank may have several first names.

When a child has the same first name as a parent, it is not uncommon to call the child by a diminutive form of the name: **Juan, Juanito; Jaime, Jaimito; Andrés, Andresito; Juana, Juanita; Laura, Laurita; Carmen, Carmencita.**

Usually, first names are the names of saints of the Catholic Church, such as **José** (Joseph), **Pedro** (Peter), **María** (Mary), and **Teresa** (Teresa). Related to this is the Hispanic custom of celebrating one's saint's day (the day on which the Church honors that saint). This could be considered the Hispanic equivilant of our celebrating birthdays.

The name **Jesús** is not uncommon for men. Since Jesus is usually referred to in Spanish as **Jesucristo,** the given name **Jesús** does not sound as strange to a Spanish speaker as it would to a speaker of English. Some Hispanic women's names are short forms of different titles given to the Virgin Mary or of events related to her: **Guadalupe** (and the derived forms **Lupe** and **Lupita)** from **Nuestra Señora de Guadalupe** (Our Lady of Guadalupe); **Rocío** from **Nuestra Señora del Rocío** (Our Lady of the Dew); **Desamparados** (and the derived form **Amparo**) from **Nuestra Señora de los Desamparados** (Our Lady of the Abandoned); **Consuelo** from **Nuestra Señora del Consuelo** (Our Lady of Consolation); **Pilar** from **Nuestra Señora del Pilar** (Our Lady of the Pillar); **Carmen** from **Nuestra Señora del Carmen** (Our Lady of [Mount] Carmel); **Inmaculada** or **Concepción** (and the derived forms **Concha** and **Conchita**) from **la Inmaculada Concepción de Nuestra Señora** (the Immaculate Conception of Our Lady).

A male might have a masculinized form of a feminine name **(Mario** from **María; Carmelo** from **Carmen)** or the feminine name itself **(Guadalupe).** Feminized forms of masculine names are common for women: **Josefa** from **José; Jesusa** and **Jesusita** from **Jesús.**

People may have compound first names: **María Elena, Pedro Ignacio, José Jaime**.

As the second part of a compound first name, men may have the name **María: José María, Antonio María**. The second name in a man's compound first name may be abbreviated: **José M.** (for **María**) Martínez, Juan C. (for **Carlos**) Martínez.

As the second part of a compound first name, women may have the name **José: María José, Isabel José**.

When the first name of a woman's compound first name is **María,** it is often shortened to **Mari** and joined with the full second part of the name or the ending of the second part of the name to form one word. In the first case, when the compound name is written, the initial letter of the second name may be capitalized or lower-cased: **MariConsuelo** or **Mariconsuelo** from **María Consuelo; MariCarmen** or **Maricarmen** from **María del Carmen**. In the second case, the part of the second name is always lower-cased: **Maribel** from **María Isabel; Marisa** from **María Luisa**.

Last names

A person's last name is his or her **apellido** (surname). The **-ez** ending of many surnames (**Álvarez, González, Martínez, Pérez, Rodríguez**) originally indicated an offspring of the person to whose name the suffix was attached; a man named **Álvarez** was the son of **Álvaro**. (This parallels the original meaning of *-son* in names like *Johnson, Ericson,* etc.)

People have two last names, usually the last name of the father followed by the last name of the mother:

> If **Juan** *García* **Grau** marries **María** *López* **Gomar**, their daughter's name will be **Ana** *García López*.

People usually use only their first last (paternal) name:

> **María Plá Martínez** would usually be simply **María Plá**.

People who have common first (paternal) last names might use both of their last names, hyphenated, at all times: **Manuel González-Salas**.

Or sometimes they may come to be known by and to use only their second (maternal) last name (except for formal or official matters): **Manuel González Salas,** instead of being called **González** or **señor González,** may be known to his friends as **Salas,** or more formally as **señor Salas.** Two well-known examples are the famous Spanish writers **Federico García Lorca,** who is known as **García Lorca;** and **Benito Pérez Galdós,** known as **Pérez Galdós** or **Galdós.**

Some people use all four of their last names, that is, both last names of the father followed by both last names of the mother: **José Jiménez-Carlés Pérez-Piñal.** This is often done to indicate distinction, nobility, or high class.

Importance of using two last names

As indicated above, people often use only one (their first) last name. Nevertheless, it is important in some instances to use both last names, lest one be considered to be of illegitimate birth. In connection with this, people from our culture need to be aware that they may be pressed to give a second last name when giving their full name. In such cases, they should consider the way their name is given on passports or other identification documents, and give their middle name as their first last name and their surname as the second last name, and be prepared to be addressed, for instance as "Miss Sandra" or "Mr. Kevin," with their middle name being taken for their first surname.

It is also important to know a person's second surname in order to be able to find the appropriate individual in a list of names, especially in a phone directory. This is due in part to the frequent usage of first names within a family. For example, a grandfather, father, and son could have the same first name and first last name; the only distinguishing feature would be the second last name, the first family name of each of their mothers. (See Point 62, "Telephone.")

Last names of married women

If **Ana García López** marries **Pedro Vega Pereda,** she is still **Ana García López.** However, she may be referred to or her name may be written in a variety of ways: **Ana; Ana García; Ana García López** (very formal); **Ana García de Vega** (which means that **Ana García** is the "wife of" **Vega**); **Ana G. de Vega** or **Ana García de Vega P.** (through the use of abbreviations, other combinations can result in local usage); **señora de Vega** (used in addressing her; *la* **señora de Vega** would be used in referring to her); **señora Ana García** (used in addressing her; *la* **señora Ana García** would be used in referring to her).

As can be seen, a woman does not use her first name followed by her husband's last name. When she uses her husband's name as part of her own, she uses her first and last name(s), the **de,** plus her husband's last name(s); his second surname may be abbreviated.

A widow who wishes to use her late husband's last name may use **Vda. (viuda,** widow) **de** (of) . . . after her own last name or the abbreviation of it: **Juana Pereda Vda. de Ramírez** or **Juana P. Vda. de Ramírez.**

Note that a woman never uses her husband's first name as part of her name; a Hispanic woman is never, for instance, Mrs. Pedro Vega. A man introducing his wife never uses his own last name as part of hers. **Sr. González** would say **Le presento a mi esposa, Ana García** (May I introduce my wife, Ana Garcia, to you).

Nicknames

Apodos

An **apodo** is a special kind of nickname, a phrase used following a person's name. It is usually taken from a personal circumstance of the person (or even a family member), such as the place of origin or residence (**el argentino,** the one who is from Argentina or who lives or has lived there, or is a relative or descendant of someone from Argentina); a physical characteristic (often one that is a defect: **el chato,** the one with the flat nose, or **el cojo,** the lame one); or a job (**el chocolatero,** the one who makes chocolate or is a descendant of one who makes or used to make it).

73

An **apodo** is a term used in referring to someone in a very informal way. However, due to its meaning or to possible implications, it might have negative overtones, and so should never be used to address or even refer to the person in his or her presence.

Nombres hipocorísticos

Another kind of nickname is a **nombre hipocorístico** (pet name), an alteration of, or a substitute for, a given name. This can be a shortening (**Rafa** for **Rafael, Lupe** for **Guadalupe, Amparo** for **Desamparados**); a diminutive (**Jaimito** for **Jaime, Carmencita** for **Carmen**); a standard alteration of a name (**Toño** for **Antonio; Quique** for **Henrique; Paco, Quico,** or **Curro** for **Francisco; Manolo** for **Manuel; Pepe**[4] for **José; Lola** or **Lolita** for **Dolores; Paca** or **Quica** for **Francisca; Pepa** for **Josefa; Pili** for **Pilar**).

In Hispanic cultures, as in ours, some people have unique, inside, homemade nicknames. These can be new words that have been created, real words or alterations of real words, or a name totally different from the person's given name. This kind of nickname can have its origin in anything from a child's inability to say a name correctly to a characteristic or an event: **Nanina** for **Carmina, Laula** for **Laura.**

name day, *día del santo*

Most Hispanic first names are the names of saints of the Catholic Church. The days that the Church has designated to honor individual saints are marked on Hispanic calendars. Although in parts of the Hispanic world people may celebrate their birthday, they more often

---

[4]One origin that has been given for the name **Pepe** is the initials *P.P.,* which are read in Spanish as **pe-pe.** These initials, which stand for the Latin phrase *pater putativus* (considered father), were at one time used following the name of **José,** the spouse of Mary, the Mother of Jesus.

celebrate their saint's day, or, if both occasions are observed, they usually place more emphasis on their saint's day.

To celebrate a child's saint's day, sometimes friends are invited to the home.

The prevalent custom is that an adult who is celebrating a saint's day treats friends and relatives who come to congratulate him or her. (Visitors are not usually invited, but are expected to drop by some time during the day or evening. On occasion, some will be invited for dinner.)

There are several terms that are used to refer to a person's saint's day or its celebration:

el santo, the saint's day (short for **el día del santo,** the day of the saint, the saint's day)

su santo, his/her/your saint's day (short for **el día de su santo,** the day of his/her/your saint, his/her/your saint's day)

su onomástico, his/her/your name day (short for **su día onomástico,** his/her/your name day)

su onomástica, his/her/your name day celebration (short for **su fiesta onomástica,** his/her/your name day celebration)

48. PHYSICAL DISTANCE AND CONTACT

When talking, when waiting somewhere, when simply standing on a bus or sitting on a park bench, people stand or sit much closer to one another than they do in our culture. Moving away from someone who seems too close to you can be considered an affront, especially if that person is talking to you.

While talking, people often use accompanying gestures and even touch the other person (on the arm, on the shoulder, with a gentle poke to the chest) or the other person's clothing.

Women often go arm in arm, as do husbands and wives.

49. *PIROPO*

A **piropo** is a complimentary but flirtatious remark addressed to a woman or women by a male passerby. A person **echando un piropo** (throwing a flattering remark) is indicating his awareness and appreciation of charm and beauty.

Usually, **piropos** should simply be ignored. They are not intended solely for the benefit of the "recipient." Many times they are made for the image they convey to others of the maker of the remark. Some examples of **piropos**:

> **¡Bendita sea la madre que te parió!**
> Bless the mother who gave birth to you!

> **¡Dios mío! ¡Tanta curva y yo sin frenos!**
> My God! So many curves and me without brakes!

> **¡Vaya Ud. con Dios y su hija conmigo!**
> May you go with God and your daughter with me!

> **¡Santa María! ¡Qué pinta trae la niña!**
> Holy Mary! What a good look the girl has!

>> (This **piropo** plays on the names of Columbus's three ships, the **Niña,** the **Pinta,** and the **Santa María.**)

50. PROFESSIONAL AND CIVIC TITLES

Much more frequently in Spanish than in English, people are addressed or referred to by a title reflecting their highest academic degree, their profession, or their job or role: **doctor/doctora Lara** (Doctor Lara), **licenciado/licenciada Pérez** (Licentiate Perez), **ingeniero/ingeniera García** (Engineer Garcia), **gerente Martínez** (Manager Martinez, both masculine and feminine).

These titles may be preceded by **señor, señora,** or **señorita.** They may be used, both with and without the person's last name, in addressing or referring to him or her, as a way of showing respect and courtesy:

señor doctor, señor doctor Lara	Dr. Lara (male)
señora doctora, señora doctora Lara	Dr. Lara (female)
señorita licenciada, señorita licenciada	
Pérez	Licentiate Perez

Note that the person's first name is not used, except perhaps in addressing the person in writing, as in a letter or on an envelope.

Licenciado/licenciada, **abbreviated** *lic.*

The holder of a **licenciatura** (degree of licentiate) may be called a **licenciado** (for a male) or **licenciada** (for a female). The degree indicates that the holder is qualified in a particular academic field:

licenciado/licenciada en química	licentiate in chemistry
licenciado/licenciada en derecho	licentiate in law

In current usage, those who hold degrees in law use their titles more frequently than those in other fields, so the title **licenciado/licenciada** often indicataes that the person is a lawyer.

ciudadano (citizen), **abbreviated** *C.*

In Mexico, the term **ciudadano,** in its abbreviated form, **C.,** is often found in newspapers before the title and name of a public official:

C. Licenciado Miguel de la Madrid (former president of Mexico)

❁

51. PUNCTUALITY

Hispanics have, in varying degrees, a perception of time that is different from ours. In many places in the Hispanic world, punctuality as we understand it is unheard of. People who have been invited for 8:00 may not begin to arrive until 8:30 or later. However, if you are invited somewhere, do not assume that you may arrive late.

It should be noted that, primarily in large cities, things are changing. Public functions, such as movies, theatrical performances, bullfights (which are noted for starting on time), and big businesses tend to run according to schedule.

❁

52. RELIGION

In the Hispanic world, religion traditionally has played a greater role in the social life and daily activity of the people than is generally the case in our culture.

At times, seemingly secular activities may begin with a mass or with some other religious manifestation, such as a blessing: a boat in a fishing fleet may be blessed; a mass may be said before a military parade or celebration; a family, or even a business or the government, may request that a mass be said because of an event significant to them; a new home may be blessed.

❁

53. RESTAURANTS

As would be expected, one can find all kinds of restaurants in the Hispanic world, from the most elegant five-star establishments to franchises of some of our fast-food chains; and from those serving European cuisine to those specializing in regional foods or those of various countries or ethnic groups.

Sidewalk cafes are much more widespread than in our country, due in part to the agreeability of the climate. It also has to do with the centrality of social life and with the fact that business is usually concentrated in the heart of the city or town rather than being scattered in malls, outlying complexes, and the like. Another factor is the general Hispanic fondness for talking to friends and, at times, even with business associates, while lingering over coffee, a soft drink, or something light to eat.

In some places, one finds a number of very small restaurants that may have room for only two or three tables. These usually cater to a neighborhood clientele, rather than to the public at large. Especially in Spain, an establishment called a "bar" is not the kind of place that comes to mind when one hears the English word *bar*. Spanish bars usually serve, in addition to alcoholic and nonalcoholic drinks, a variety of **tapas** (hors d'oeuvres), many of which are attractively displayed in glass cases that run the length of the counter at which patrons sit. (See Point 40, "Meals and mealtimes.") It is not uncommon for bars to have a restaurant area that serves everything from sandwiches or desserts to full meals.

A **cafetería** means just a café, not a cafeteria as we think of it—a restaurant where one pushes a tray along a track and makes selections while passing by the different food items.

Cafes, indoor or outdoor, traditionally have been the meeting places for social, political, and literary **tertulias.** (See Point 63, "**Tertulia.**") In restaurants in the Hispanic world, everything is usually served à la carte. In some places, however, there can be a complete meal, perhaps the special of the day, that might be called **comida corriente** or **cubierto.** This meal is less expensive than it would be if all its components were ordered à la carte.

Note that the word **cubierto** can mean several different things: a full meal, as above; the table service, or place setting, which in the Hispanic world consists of plate, knife, fork, spoon, bread, and napkin; or a cover charge.

54. ROLES

Traditional roles, and people's views of them, are changing in varying degrees in different countries, regions, and metropolitan areas, to the point that generalizations are no longer possible.

As industrialized society advances, more and more women are entering the work force in both professional and nonprofessional fields.

However, certain traditional roles for middle- and upper-class men and women are still prevalent to a great degree. A man's world is out of the house: going to work, attending male social gatherings. A woman's world is at home: running the house, directing the help, if any, and rearing the children. Traditionally, men never help in the dining room or the kitchen. Doing such things as clearing the table or washing the dishes is considered "women's work."

The upbringing of girls and of boys differs. Girls are generally trained to be passive, sentimental, humble, and submissive. Boys are generally brought up to be the opposite, and are allowed, both as children and as young men, freedom and behavior that would never be tolerated in a girl or a young woman.

In spite of the changing situations and attitudes, women's lives remain restricted. In most places, for instance, a woman traveling alone or seen out alone at night might be looked upon with raised eyebrows.

❁

55. *SEÑOR, SEÑORA, SEÑORITA*

Señor, señora, and **señorita** are titles of courtesy. They are written in lower case in the middle of a sentence:

Buenos días, señor García.

Señor, señora, and señorita are often abbreviated. The abbreviations are capitalized at all times:

señor, Sr.   señor García, Sr. García
señora, Sra.   señora García, Sra. García
señorita, Srta.   señorita García, Srta. García

Usage of *señor, señora, señorita*

Each of the three can be used alone, with no name following, in order to attract attention:

¡Señor!   ¡Señora!   ¡Señorita!

Each of the three can be used with a person's last name (first name may be included), in addressing or referring to that person:

señor García   Mr. Garcia
señora Ana Pereda   Mrs. Ana Pereda
señorita Fernández   Miss Fernandez

Each of the three can be used with a person's title or with the name of his or her job or profession (but not followed by the person's name) to show courtesy when calling, addressing, or referring to the person.

Sr. profesor   male professor
Sr. guardia   policeman
Sra. directora   principal (a married woman)
Srta. maestra   teacher (a single woman)
Sra. doctora   female doctor
Sr. ingeniero   male engineer

Señor and señora are used with only a first name to address or refer to older people, in order to show a degree of respect, but doing so indicates the lower social status of the person addressed:

Speaking about the person:	Calling the person:
nuestra criada, la señora Juana our maid, señora Juana	Juana or señora Juana
el portero, el señor Juan the doorman, señor Juan	Juan or señor Juan

Señor may be used to refer to the man of the house:

El señor no está en casa.
The **señor** (man of the house) isn't in.

Señora may be used:

in addressing or referring to a married woman of any age.

in addressing or referring to any woman of middle age or older, who is a stranger and whose marital status is not known.

in addressing or referring to the woman of the house, regardless of age:

La señora no está.
The **señora** (woman of the house) isn't in.

with the meaning of *Mrs., wife:*

la señora de Pérez	Mrs. Perez (the wife of Perez)
Recuerdos a tu señora.	Best regards to your wife.

Señores, besides being used to express *sirs, gentlemen, ladies and gentlemen,* can be used for *Mr. and Mrs.:*

los señores García   Mr. and Mrs. Garcia

Señorita may be used:

in addressing or referring to any young woman who is single.

in addressing or referring to any young woman whose marital status is not known, as a stranger.

in addressing or referring to any single woman, regardless of age, followed by her first name only, as a title of respect paralleling **doña.** (See Point 21, "**Don, doña.**")

by a maid, in referring to the woman of the house, whether married or single:

La señorita no está en casa.
The **señorita** isn't home.

in referring to a daughter of the house, in which case it is followed by the girl's or woman's first name:

La señorita María no está en casa.
Señorita Maria isn't in.

to convey the idea of a young woman who is idle, lazy, and useless.

Juana es una señorita.
Juana is a "señorita" (lazy thing).

La muy señorita no quiere hacer nada.
The very "señorita" (lazy thing) doesn't want to do anything.

The title *señorito*

Grammatically, **señorito** is the masculine counterpart of **señorita,**
but **señorito** is limited in application and is used less frequently.

Señorito may be used:

in referring to the man of the house:

> **El señorito no está en casa.**
> The **señorito** isn't home.

by the maid in referring to a son of the house, in which case it is
followed by the boy's or man's first name:

> **El señorito Andrés no está en casa.**
> **Señorito** Andres isn't home.

to convey the idea of a young man who is idle, lazy, and useless.

> **Juan es un señorito.**
> Juan is a "señorito" (lazy thing).

> **El muy señorito no quiere hacer nada.**
> The very "señorito" (lazy thing) doesn't want to do anything.

56. SHOPPING

In our country, we can go to a supermarket and find all the groceries
we need under one roof, including many convenience foods that are
packaged, processed, or frozen. In the Hispanic world, supermarkets
are becoming common in large cities (they are called **supermercados**

in Spanish America and **hipermercados** in Spain), but in towns, nearly everything is sold fresh, and a shopper might have to go to a different store or to a separate stall in the market for each item: to a **huevería** for eggs and chicken, to a **carnicería** for meat, to a **panadería** for bread, to a **pescadería** for fish, to a **verdulería** for fruits and vegetables, and to a **salchichonería** for sausages.

In some places, people must go to the market early in the morning to buy items that are in short supply, such as meat and milk, or just to get the best of what is available.

In some places, there are somewhat larger grocery stores that carry a variety of items. These are known by different names in different places: **tienda de comestibles, tienda de abarrotes, tienda de víveres, bodega,** or **colmado.**

In Spain, you can find the **tienda de ultramarinos,** which originally specialized in imported nonperishable food items, such as spices, canned goods, and cured meats, that came primarily from the Americas or from Asia.

Markets

Many towns and even larger cities have a big centralized market where vendors sell various food items and other wares. Some are open-air street markets; others are enclosed.

It is common for a town to have a special market day, when people from outlying areas sell their products, which can include produce, housewares, clothing, items they have made, and, in rural areas, animals. These market days are of special interest to tourists in areas noted for local crafts. The markets are usually held in streets and plazas, often as an extension of the regular daily market.

Pharmacies and drugstores

Farmacias (pharmacies) sell only prescription and nonprescription drugs and medications. In pharmacies in the Hispanic world, one can buy without prescription many items, such as antibiotics, for which one would need a prescription in our country.

Drugstores are usually not like those in the U.S., where one can buy small electrical appliances, toys, stationery and greeting cards, hardware items, foods, plants, cameras, and so on. **Droguerías** are technically for selling chemicals and chemical products, which could include chlorine, peroxide, paint, rug cleaner, soap, and beauty items such as perfume, hair coloring products, nail polish and remover, and the like. They also sell items related to the use or application of these products, such as paintbrushes, facial tissues, and cotton balls.

Bookstores

Bookstores in the Hispanic world are generally fewer in number and are often more literarily and intellectually oriented than in the U.S. There don't seem to be as many new books coming out all the time, as we are used to, on topics like gardening, diet, exercise, beating stress, house remodeling, and running a business.

Bargaining or not

In some places, bargaining is expected, such as in an open-air market; in others, such as department stores and supermarkets, where there are **precios fijos** (fixed prices), there is no bargaining. Small shops for tourists generally have fixed prices, but may on occasion give a discount or a special price.

Bargaining should be done only if there is a sincere interest in buying; otherwise, it could be offensive.

Some commonly used expressions are:

> **¿Cuál es su mejor precio?**
> What is your best price?

> **¿Es eso su mejor precio?**
> Is that your best price?

Selecting and paying for a purchase

Most stores are specialty shops, with one category of related items for sale. In such shops, and in open markets, you should ask for or indicate what you want, but never touch or pick up an item without permission.

When a purchase is decided upon, it is common for the salesperson not to take the customer's money. Instead, he or she will take the item to a cashier (**cajero/cajera**) at the place where you pay (**caja**), which could be right at the person's elbow. The customer pays the cashier, then receives the merchandise. In places where food is sold, it is not uncommon for prospective buyers to sample something, such as a grape.

Window shopping

Many vendors and retailers in small shops don't quite understand our concept of window shopping. They feel that people go shopping to buy something they need, and don't see how they can be looking, with no specific purpose, at items for sale. Therefore, casual browsers are often treated in what they might consider a brusque manner, for they are viewed as uselessly taking up the time of the vendor or clerk.

❁

57. SMALL TALK

Small talk between strangers should be limited to very general, impersonal topics, such as the beauty of the countryside, sports (in a very general way), and other noncontroversial matters. Questions about where someone is from or what he or she does, or inquiries about his or her family can be taken as intrusive. In our culture, weather is one of the major topics for small talk, but this is rarely the case in the Hispanic world.

❁

58. SPAIN'S NEW POLITICAL DIVISIONS (*COMUNIDADES AUTÓNOMAS*)

In 1978, the traditional regions (**regiones tradicionales**) of Spain were granted autonomy, and with this came some adjustments in their political boundaries, as can be seen by comparing the following two maps.

Regiones tradicionales

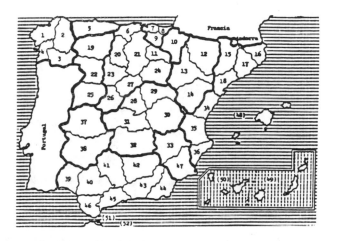

Comunidades autónomas

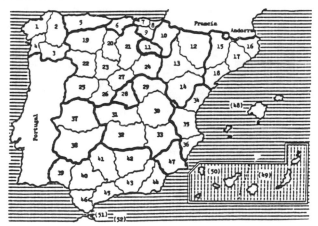

The new **comunidades autónomas** brought about a renaissance in regionalism and in the regional tongues of **gallego** in Galicia, **catalán** in Catalonia, **valenciano** in Valencia, **mallorquín** in the Balearic Islands, and **vascuence** in the Basque Provinces. Historically, Spain has been referred to as **las Españas,** due to the strong ties Spaniards have with the region from which they come. The new autonomous regions and emphasis on the individual characteristics of the **comunidades autónomas** lend continuing support to regional pride.

Regiones tradicionales	Provincias
Andalucía	Huelva (39), Sevilla (40), Córdoba (41), Jaén (42), Granada (43), Almería (44), Málaga (45), Cádiz (46)
Aragón	Zaragoza (13), Huesca (12), Teruel (14)
Asturias	Asturias (5)
Baleares	Baleares (48)
Canarias	Santa Cruz de Tenerife (50), Las Palmas (49)
Castilla la Nueva	Madrid (28), Toledo (31), Ciudad Real (32), Cuenca (30), Guadalajara (29)
Castilla la Vieja	Santander (6), Logroño (11), Burgos (21), Valladolid (23), Palencia (20), Soria (24), Segovia (27), Ávila (26)
Cataluña	Barcelona (17), Tarragona (18), Lérida (15), Gerona (16)
Extremadura	Cáceres (37), Badajoz (38)
Galicia	La Coruña (1), Lugo (2), Orense (3), Pontevedra (4)
León	León (19), Zamora (22), Salamanca (25)
Murcia	Albacete (33), Murcia (47)
Navarra	Navarra (10)
Provincias Vascongadas	Vizcaya (7), Álava (9), Guipúzcoa (8)
Valencia	Valencia (35), Castellón de la Plana (34), Alicante (36)

Comunidades autónomas	*Capitales*/Provincias
Andalucía	*Sevilla,* Huelva (39), Sevilla (40), Córdoba (41), Jaén (42), Granada (43), Almería (44), Málaga (45), Cádiz (46)
Aragón	*Zaragoza,* Zaragoza (13), Huesca (12), Teruel (14)
Asturias	*Oviedo,* Asturias (5)
Baleares	*Palma de Mallorca,* Baleares (48)
Canarias	*Las Palmas de Gran Canaria,* Santa Cruz de Tenerife (50), Las Palmas (49)
Cantabria	*Santander,* Santander (6)
Castilla-La Mancha	*Toledo,* Albacete (33), Toledo (31), Ciudad Real (32), Cuenca (30), Guadalajara (29)
Castilla y León	*Valladolid,* Zamora (22), Segovia (27), Palencia (20), Burgos (21), Valladolid (23), Soria (24), Salamanca (25), Ávila (26), León (19)
Cataluña	*Barcelona,* Barcelona (17), Tarragona (18), Lérida (15), Gerona (16)
Extremadura	*Mérida,* Cáceres (37), Badajoz (38)
Galicia	*Santiago de Compostela,* La Coruña (1), Lugo (2), Orense (3), Pontevedra (4)
La Rioja	*Logroño,* Logroño (11)
Madrid	*Madrid,* Madrid (28)
Murcia	*Murcia,* Murcia (47)
Navarra	*Pamplona,* Navarra (10)
País Valenciano	*Valencia,* Valencia (35), Castellón de la Plana (34), Alicante (36)
País Vasco	*Vitoria,* Vizcaya (7), Guipúzcoa (8), Álava (9)
Ciudades africanas	Ceuta (51), Melilla (52)

59. SPORTS

Although all sports are practiced to one degree or another in the Hispanic world, the most popular spectator sports are **fútbol** (soccer), **baloncesto** (basketball), **béisbol** (baseball), **boxeo** (boxing), **ciclismo** (cycling), and, in Mexico, Cuba, and Spain, **jai alai.** The most popular participation sports are **fútbol** (soccer), **baloncesto** (basketball), **béisbol** (baseball), **frontón** (handball), and **ciclismo** (cycling). Soccer is undoubtedly the most popular and important of all sports, except perhaps in the Caribbean Islands, Central America, and Venezuela, where baseball is extremely popular. Spontaneously organized games, which in the U.S. might be softball or football, usually are soccer games in the Hispanic world.

Sports competitions among schools are not as common as in our country. Many local sports clubs compete, mainly in soccer. In the countries where cycling is especially popular, such as Spain and Colombia, there are annual competitions called **la vuelta a** (name of country)—**la vuelta a España** (the tour of Spain) and **la vuelta a Colombia** (the tour of Colombia).

There are several well-known ski areas in Argentina and Chile. The Chacaltaya slopes, near La Paz, Bolivia, are the highest in the world. **Jai alai** (Basque for **juego de pelota,** ball game), also called **pelota vasca** (Basque ball) or just **pelota**, is a unique sport that comes from the Basque country in Spain.

Some claim that **jai alai** is a descendant of *tlachtli,* the Aztec game that they believe Cortes imported to Spain from Mexico. However, since the king of Castile, Philip I, died from injuries incurred while playing **pelota** in 1501, thirteen years before Cortes reached Mexico, this theory seems not to have merit.

Jai alai is also played in major Spanish cities, in Mexico, where it is one of the most popular spectator sports, in Cuba, and in Florida in the U.S. In the Basque region, it is played year round; in the rest of Spain there are daily games during the season, which runs from October to June. **Jai alai** is something like handball, and is one of the fastest and most skill-demanding games ever devised. It is usually played between two teams of two players each. The players use a **cesta,** a long, scooplike wicker basket that is strapped to one hand, to catch the extremely hard ball and hurl it against the wall **(frontis).**

Jai alai is played in a long, three-walled court called a **frontón.** The fourth side, one of the long ones, is made of wire mesh, which protects spectators from the ball, which can reach speeds of up to 100 miles an hour. The largest **frontón** in the world is in Miami, Florida, and seats 5,100 spectators. (The place where handball is played is also called a **frontón.)**

60. STARING

In the Hispanic world, people may unabashedly stare at others. This may not only attract the attention of the foreigner but may cause a degree of discomfort or even annoyance. There are not necessarily any specific reasons or intentions involved besides simple curiosity about the strangers in their midst. Foreigners who feel that they are being stared at should neither take offense nor feel that they are being singled out. In most instances, staring is just a common reaction to someone or something new.

61. STREET NAMES AND ADDRESSES

In the Hispanic world, it is not uncommon for streets to be given names of important dates in a country's history, of political or military figures in its past, of famous writers, painters, or other artists, or of saints. In Mexico, for instance, **Cinco de mayo**[5] (May fifth) is not an uncommon street name. (In the U.S., we probably would not name a street *Fourth of July.* We do, however, name streets after presi-

---

[5]**Cinco de mayo** (May 5). On this date in 1867 the Mexican army defeated troops led by the French general Laurencez. The French were fighting on behalf of Emperor Maximilian, an Austrian who had been sent by Napoleon III of France to rule Mexico. The Mexican victory is an event that is commemorated and celebrated.

dents and other people of note, and many streets are named for trees, flowers, and fruits, something that is not customary in the Hispanic world.)

Addresses

As appropriate, the items in an address are written as follows:

street, street number, floor number, apartment number (The apartment number is really the number of the door, as is seen in the examples.)

Calle 5 de mayo, 28, 2°, 3ª

or

5 de mayo, 28, 2°, 3ª (The use of **calle** is optional.)

The street name is a date (May 5); the building number is 28; the floor number is 2 (**2°** for **segundo piso,** second floor); the apartment or office number, really the door number, is 3 (**3ª** for **tercera puerta,** third door).

Avda. Stos. Patronos, 12, 4°, 8ª

or

Stos. Patronos, 12, 4°, 8ª

(**Avda.** is the abbreviation of **Avenida; Stos.** is the abbreviation of **Santos. Santos Patronos** means *Patron Saints.*)

The street name is **Avenida Santos Patronos;** the building number is 12; the floor number is 4; the apartment or office number, really the door number, is 8.

If no door number is given after the floor, it indicates that the apartment or office occupies the entire floor.

In urban areas in the Hispanic world, each floor of a high-rise apartment building may have only one or two large apartments. In numbering the doors within a building, it is possible that the numbers begin with *1* at the lowest floor where the numbering is used, then continue from floor to floor, rather than beginning at *1* on each floor. In the last address given above, for instance, since the office door number is *8* on the fourth floor, one might assume that doors 1 and 2 are on the first floor, 3 and 4 on the second floor, 5 and 6 on the third floor, and 7 and 8 on the fourth floor.

An address can be ''corner'' of two streets. This is because many corners are **esquinas achaflanadas** (cut-off corners) and entrances are on **el chaflán** (the cut-off).

> **Esquina Calderón de la Barca y Avenida Santos Patronos**
> Corner Calderon de la Barca and Santos Patronos Avenue
>
> or
>
> **Calderón de la Barca, esquina Avenida Santos Patronos**
> Calderon de la Barca, corner Santos Patronos Avenue

This way of giving an address indicates that technically the street number is on **Calderón de la Barca.** But because the address is on a **chaflán,** it is easier to give the name of the intersection than just the number.

Generally, the numbers in street addresses are low; it is not common to have four- or five-digit numbers. This is because buildings are just numbered in sequence along a street, not the way it is done in most places in the U.S., where buildings between, for example, the eighth and ninth cross streets are given numbers in the eight hundreds (making that the eight hundred block), and buildings between the twenty-third and twenty-fourth cross streets are numbered in the twenty-three hundreds (the twenty-three hundred block).

An address may give just the street name followed by **s/n** (**sin número,** without number), where, for any reason, the residences and businesses have not been given numbers.

❁

62. TELEPHONE

Answering the phone

People answer the phone differently in different places. **¡Diga . . . !**, **¡Dígame . . . !**, and **¡Aló!** might be heard or used anywhere. Following are some ways they answer the phone in different parts of the Hispanic world: **¡Diga . . . !** and **¡Dígame . . . !** in Spain; **¡Bueno!** in Mexico; **¿Qué hay?** and **¡Oigo!** in Cuba; **¡A ver!** in Colombia; **¡Holá!** in Argentina and Uruguay; **¡Sí . . . !** in Venezuela; **¡Aló!** in Peru, Ecuador, and most other places; **¡Al habla . . . !** and **¡Al aparato!** in several places.

Phone directory

In many places, especially in Mexico City, people do not list their phones in the directory.

In phone directories in the Hispanic world, names are alphabetized by people's first (paternal) last names. In looking up someone's phone number, it is very important to know both of that person's last names, as there can be pages of listings of people with the same first last name, and multiple entries of people with the same first and last names. This comes in part from the fact that parents often give their firstborn, especially a son, their own first name. So there can be a grandfather, father, and son with the same first and last name. For example, all three might be named **Juan García,** and their mothers' last names would be the distinguishing features in their full names. (See Point 47, ''People's names and name day.'')

Long-distance calls

In some places, when you want to place a long-distance call, it is necessary to go to the main office (or a branch office) of the telephone company, where a phone booth is assigned to you and the call is placed by an operator. When the call is concluded, you go to the desk and pay the charges.

❏

63. *TERTULIA*

A **tertulia** is a gathering of people who meet, usually every day, to linger over coffee (and perhaps an after-dinner drink) and to talk. Those in attendance discuss a given topic (politics, sports, current events, literature) or just have friendly conversation. **Tertulias** are held in cafés or bars.

The three characteristics of a **tertulia** are:

constancy in people (same group of friends);
constancy in locale (same place always);
constancy in time (same time of day, year in and year out).

An interesting note about the origin of **tertulias** is found in John Crow's *Spain: The Root and the Flower*[6]:

Among the social pastimes of the eighteenth century was one which has since become almost the distinguishing mark of Spanish life, the **tertulia,** or conversational gathering. The name itself originally referred to a restricted part of the theaters which was reserved for serious-minded men, many of them priests who enjoyed talking about Tertullian.[7] Hence, their part of the theater was called the **tertulia.** Later, the term came to mean any session of men, or women, or of mixed company in which conversation held the floor. There were also literary **tertulias** at which the writers gathered. Later still, each individual writer of note had his own **tertulia** which was attended by his admirers and disciples. This custom still prevails today. These literary **tertulias** always gather at a certain cafe on a given day of the week, and the address is even better known to the author's friends than that of his home.

---

[6]Crow, John. *Spain: The Root and the Flower.* 3rd ed. Berkeley, CA: University of California Press, 1985, p. 237.

[7]Tertullian (Quintus Septimius Florens Tertullianus), ca. 150–230, was a Christian theologian of the Roman Empire, who was born in Carthage.

64. TESTS

In general, in Spanish-speaking countries, on both the high school and college levels, there are fewer tests during the year. The final examinations, which may include both oral and written parts, carry a great deal of weight and, in some instances, may be the sole deciding factor determining a student's course grade.

Oral tests are given to each student individually by a panel of examiners called a **tribunal.**

Cheating on tests is viewed differently in Hispanic countries than it is in our culture. (See Point 23, ''Education.'') Teachers might punish those who are caught cheating, but there is no deep feeling that moral wrongdoing has occurred. From the point of view of the students, it is almost a game or a show of skill to be able to outsmart the teacher in cheating and its techniques.

65. TIME OF DAY

When the time is written in Spanish, a period or a comma is used between the hour and the minutes, instead of a colon.

El tren sale el jueves a las 3.15 (or **3,15).**
The train leaves on Thursday at 3:15.

Since Spanish speakers usually don't use an equivalent of A.M. or P.M., in printed timetables, schedules, and the like, the twenty-four-hour clock is used to avoid confusion.

El tren sale a las 14.30 (catorce treinta).
The train leaves at 2:30 P.M.

Generally, in other situations, the twenty-four-hour clock isn't used.

La reunión es a las 2.30 (dos y media).
The meeting is at 2:30.

To figure out time on a twenty-four-hour clock, if the hour given is after twelve, merely subtract twelve from it.

14.25 is 2:25 p.m.

Since the advent of digital clocks and watches, it has become more common to hear people telling the time with phrases like **tres cuarenta** (three forty) rather than the more traditional **cuatro menos veinte** (four minus twenty).

❁

66. *TÚ* AND *USTED, VOSOTROS* AND *USTEDES*

Uses of *tú*

The use of **tú** is called **tuteo;** to use **tú** with someone is **tutear. Tú** is used in informal address with friends, family, pets, and sometimes with household help.

Tú may be used to create an atmosphere of closeness and dignity when **usted** would be too distant, as in praying to God and saints, and addressing the king, other members of royalty, or high-ranking officials:

Tú, que eres nuestro Señor, . . .
You, who are our Lord, . . .

Usted and *ustedes*

The abbreviation for **usted** is **Ud.;** the abbreviation for **ustedes** (the plural form of **usted**) is **Uds.**

Usted (you) comes from the Old Spanish word **vusted,** which stood for **vuestra merced** (your grace). This explains why the verb form used with **usted** is in the third person; the one being spoken to is technically not being addressed, but is being spoken about, as a third person, ''your grace.''

Uses of *usted* and *ustedes*

Usted is used in formal address, in all other cases when **tú** would not be used.

In some families, **usted** is used by children in speaking to their parents. It is also used by children and young adults in speaking to older people who are friends of their parents.

Most Spanish-speaking people (in Spanish America and in southern Spain, in the region of Andalusia) prefer **ustedes** as the plural of **tú.**

Tú vs. *usted*

If **tú** is expected and **usted** is used, a distance that can offend is created. If **usted** is expected and **tú** is used, it could be considered an insult, a way of putting someone down or "in his or her place." The mere reversal of **tú** and **usted** gets the message across:

To a stranger who is sitting on your car you might say:

¿Qué haces ahí?   What are you doing there? (using the **tú** form)

To a child who has misbehaved, you might say, without changing your tone of voice:

¿Qué hizo usted?   What did you do?

Because of the cultural shock for Hispanics who hear **tú** when **usted** should be used, as a practical rule, if you have the slightest doubt whether to use **tú** or **usted,** you should use **usted.** If the person wishes you to use **tú,** he or she will quickly indicate that.

Vosotros/vosotras

Vosotros (feminine **vosotras**) is the grammatical plural of **tú.** However, most Spanish-speaking people (in Spanish America and in the region of Andalusia) use **ustedes** as the plural of **tú. Vosotros** comes from **vos** (you) and **otros** (others). (See Point 68, "**Vos.**")

As with **tú, vosotros/vosotras** may be used also to create an atmosphere of closeness and dignity when **ustedes** would be too distant, as in addressing a legislative body, a congregation, and some audiences. In Spain, in the southern region of Andalusia, in very familiar situations in which **ustedes** alone would appear too formal, it is not uncommon to hear **ustedes vosotros,** followed by the third person plural **(ustedes)** form of the verb.

67. VISITING

The **visita** (visit) is an almost universal pastime for adults in the Hispanic world. Family members and friends drop in on each other, unannounced, to chat for a while, especially on Sundays and holidays. Due to the spontaneity of some **visitas,** they can be very brief, only a few minutes in length, and very informal.

Food and drink are usually not expected or offered.

68. *VOS*

Vos is an old form of respect that was the equivalent of both **usted** and **ustedes.** In the past, **vos** was widely used. Today, it is used only ocassionally in speech—to pray to God and saints, or to address, with emphatic respect, persons of high authority. In writing, **vos** is used in some documents and in poetry.

The use of **vos** is called **voseo;** to use **vos** with someone is **vosear.**

Formal use of *vos*

Formally, **vos** is used with the **vosotros** form of the verb, with either a singular or plural meaning, depending on the subject(s) to whom **vos** refers. Any accompanying adjective agrees with the person(s) addressed, as seen in the examples on the following page.

Vos, don Pedro, sois generoso.
You, don Pedro, are generous.

Vos, señores, sois generosos.
You, gentlemen, are generous.

When **vos** used formally is the subject of a reflexive verb, the relexive pronoun used is **os**.

Vos, don Pedro, os acordáis de mí.
You, don Pedro, remember me.

Vos, señores, ya os podéis retirar.
You, gentlemen, now can retire.

Informal use of *vos*

Informally, **vos** is used in popular language as a substitute for **tú,** especially in parts of Spanish America, mainly Argentina and Uruguay.

As a substitute for **tú, vos** is used with the **vosotros** form of the verb without the *i* in the diphthongs *ai* and *ei,* but with singular meaning. Any accompanying adjective is in the singular.

Vos estás cansada.   (está[i]s)
You are tired.

Vos no tenés tiempo.   (tené[i]s)
You don't have time.

Vos dijistes.   (dijiste[i]s)
You said.

When **vos** used informally is the subject of a reflexive verb, the reflexive pronoun used is **te**.

Vos te acordás de mí.
You remember me.

¿Vos te sentís mejor?
Do you feel better?

❈

69. WAITING IN LINE

In or at such places as banks, stores, ticket windows, and bus stops, where people have to wait for their turn to be helped or to board, Hispanics often don't form an orderly line. They tend to just group around the focal point, then wait their turn.

❈

70. WAY OF CONVEYING INFORMATION

Different cultures have different ways of organizing and expressing ideas, according to their own way of thinking. Speakers of Spanish and English differ in both organization and expression of ideas. Hispanics tend to be verbose and to get sidetracked, often elaborating on topics extraneous to the subject at hand. Discourse patterns, when represented by diagrams, are as shown here:

speakers of English   **speakers of Spanish**

It is not uncommon to hear phrases such as **como estaba diciendo** (as I was saying) and **volviendo a lo que decía antes** (going back to what I was saying before), which of course reflect the speaker's recognition of his or her digression.

101

POINT 70

While admittedly the following quote is the ultimate in exaggeration, it is still illustrative of the Hispanic way of conveying information. Pritchett[8] brings the following fragment of a conversation heard at customs at the Hendaye railroad station on the French-Spanish border, and the commentary on it.

> Suppose you see them, tell them I am here, but if not, not; you may not actually see them, but talk to them on the telephone perhaps, or send a message by someone else and if not on Wednesday, well then on Tuesday or Monday, if you have the car you could run over and choose your day and say you saw me, you met me on the station, and I said, if you had some means of sending them a message or you saw them, that I might come over, on Friday, say, or Saturday at the end of the week, say Sunday. Or not. If I come there I come, but if not, we shall see, so that supposing you see them. . . .
>
> This was to say, "If you go over to see them on Wednesday tell them I have arrived and will come at the end of the week."

---

[8]Pritchett, V. S. *Spanish Temper.* New York: Harper & Row, Publishers, 1965, pp. 7–8.

71. WEIGHTS AND MEASURES

Common units of measurement

1 centímetro .3937 of an inch *(less than half an inch)*
1 metro 39.37 inches *(about 1 yard and 3 inches)*
1 kilómetro = 1.000 metros .6213 of a mile *(about 5/8 of a mile)*
1 gramo .03527 of an ounce
100 gramos 3.52 ounces *(a little less than 1/4 of a pound)*
500 gramos = 1 libra 17.63 ounces *(about 1.1 pounds)*
1.000 gramos = 1 kilo = 2 libras 35.27 ounces *(about 2.2 pounds)*
1 litro 1.0567 quarts *(a fraction over a quart, liquid)*

Conversion tables

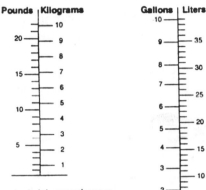

A kilogram is slightly more than two pounds (2.205 pounds).

A liter is a little more than 1/4 of a gallon, that is, a little more than a quart.

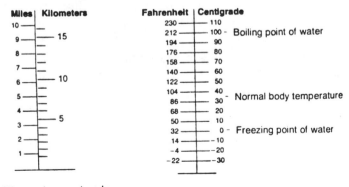

A kilometer is approximately 5/8 of a mile.

103

72. WORDS WITH MULTIPLE MEANINGS AS A SOURCE OF MISUNDERSTANDING

Many Spanish words have more than one meaning, and these meanings may be quite varied and different. With words of this kind, in some parts of the Hispanic world, one meaning may have become predominant, while in other regions, another meaning may have become the standard.

One example is the word **pieza.** In the *Diccionario de la lengua española* (*Dictionary of the Spanish Language*) of the Royal Spanish Academy, the first of the eighteen meanings given for **pieza** is "piece or part of anything"; the seventh is "any room of a house."

When a Spaniard hears **pieza,** the meaning that first comes to mind is "piece, part"; to those in other parts of the Spanish-speaking world, the primary definition is "room." One can imagine the momentary confusion (to say the least) for a Spaniard who hears a Spanish American say **Vaya a la pieza** (Go to the **pieza**).

But simple confusion can turn into shock and embarrassment, when a speaker discovers that a word that he or she has used with one meaning has as its standard local meaning another of the accepted dictionary definitions, but one that has a sexual connotation that in local parlance has become an off-color word.

There are also words in Spanish, as in other languages, that have taken on meanings totally unrelated to standard dictionary definitions and that have either a sexual or an insulting connotation. It is important to note that there are quite a few words of this kind in the Spanish lexicon, with the result that many common, everyday words have local meanings that can cause misunderstanding and embarrassment between speakers.

A person who discovers that he or she has made a lexical faux pas should not be too flustered. People are understanding of outsiders (including native speakers of Spanish from other regions) who find themselves in such a situation.

73. WORK

As in our culture, more and more women of the upper and middle classes are taking jobs and pursuing careers. Generally speaking, in the Hispanic world, women usually do not hold some jobs that are traditionally considered women's in the U.S. For example, bank tellers and bus and taxi drivers are usually men; in restaurants, one infrequently sees a waitress.

Jobs with the government and in banks, because of the greater job security and the opportunities for advancement that they provide, are highly sought after.

It is not uncommon to find several people involved in a work task that one alone could handle easily. In even a small store, one person might open a showcase to let a customer see an item, another might write up the sale, with yet a third taking the money and giving the customer the purchase. In addition to the driver (**conductor** or **chofer**), buses often have a **cobrador,** who is responsible for collecting fares.

Historically, there is scorn for manual labor in Hispanic culture. Generally speaking, a person of the middle or upper class would not want to be seen doing any sort of manual work.

In *Trato de Argel*, **Jornada 2,**[9] Cervantes makes fun of the Spaniards' attitude, which gave an advantage to their adversaries, the Moors, in naval skirmishes. He puts the following words in the mouth of a Moor from Argel, who is being pursued by Spaniards:

> **Nosotros, a la ligera**
> **listos, vivos como el fuego;**
> **y en dándonos caza, luego**
> **pico al viento y ropa fuera.**
> **. . . hacemos nuestra vía**
> **contra el viento sin trabajo;**
> **y el soldado más lucido,**
> **el más flaco y más membrudo,**
> **luego se muestra desnudo**

---

[9]Diaz-Plaja, Fernando. *El español y los siete pecados capitales.* Madrid: Alianza Editorial, 1975, p. 277.

y del bogavante asido.
Pero allá tiene la honra
el cristiano en tal extremo,
que asir en un trance el remo,
le parece que es deshonra;
y mientras ellos allá
en sus trece están honrados,
nosotros, de ellos cargados,
venimos sin honra acá.

We, in a flash
ready, alive like fire;
and when they chase us, right away
face to the wind and clothes off.
. . . we go on our way
against the wind effortlessly;
and the most dashing soldier,
the weakest and most muscular,
right away appears stripped
and grasping the oar at the lead position.
But over there has his honor
the Christian to such an extreme,
that to grasp the oar in a critical moment,
to him seems that it is a dishonor;
and while they over there
are stubborn in their pride,
we, loaded with them,
come here without honor.

In the eighteenth century, the Spanish king, Carlos III (1716–1788) issued a decree informing the people that manual work was not dishonorable and that doing it presented no obstacle to being a marquis, for example. According to Fernando Díaz-Plaja,[10] the decree did no good.

---

[10]Ibid.

SOURCES AND RELATED READINGS

Americas 1988: The Datebook of the Americas 1988. Washington, DC: Organization of American States.

Béjar, Narvarro, Raúl. *El mexicano, aspectos culturales y psico-sociales.* Mexico: Universidad Nacional Autónoma de México, 1981.

Bordón, Teresa, et al. *Atlas Turístico de España.* Barcelona: Editorial Tania, S.A.

"Building Bridges of Understanding with the Peoples of Latin America." Center for International and Area Studies. Provo: Brigham Young University, 1981.

Cottrell, John, and the Editors of Time-Life Books. *Mexico City.* Amsterdam: TIME-LIFE International (Nederland) B.V., 1979.

Crow, John. *Spain: The Root and the Flower,* 3rd ed. Berkeley: University of California Press, 1985.

"Culturegrams." Center for International and Area Studies. Provo: Brigham Young University, 1983.

Díaz-Plaja, Fernando. *El español y los siete pecados capitales.* Madrid: Alianza Editorial, 1975.

"España: Building Bridges of Understanding with the Peoples of Spain." Language and Intercultural Research Center. Provo: Brigham Young University, 1977.

Encyclopaedia Britannica. Chicago: Helen Hemingway Benton, Publisher, 1982.

Garcia, Jorge W., ed. "Culture Capsules." Wyoming, MI: PAE Publications, Inc., 1984.

Gómez de Cádiz, Javier. *Diccionario de siglas.* Barcelona: Editorial Atlas.

Gómez-Tabanera, José Manuel, ed. *El folklore español.* Madrid: Instituto Español de Antropología Aplicada, 1968.

"Intercultural Communication." Center for International and Area Studies. Provo: Brigham Young University, 1982.

Introduction to the Latin American Nations. Washington, DC: The Department of Information and Public Affairs, Organization of American States, 1970.

Lea, Tom. *Bullfight Manual for Spectators.* El Paso, TX: Carl Hertzog, 1952.

Marks, John. *To the Bullfight.* New York: Alfred A. Knopf, 1953.

Michener, James A. *Iberia: Spanish Travels and Reflections.* New York: Random House, 1968.

Norman, James. *Terry's Guide to Mexico.* Garden City, NY: Doubleday & Company, Inc., 1972.

Pritchett, V. S. *The Spanish Temper.* New York: Harper and Row, Publishers, 1965.

INDEX

INDEX

110

About the Authors

Judith Noble and **Jaime Lacasa** have published extensively on Hispanic topics and are the authors of several textbooks, reference books, and articles, including *The Complete Handbook of Spanish Verbs*, also published by Passport Books. Professors Noble and Lacasa teach in the Department of Foreign Languages and Literatures at Iowa State University.